Morocco exists in the minds of most Americans and Europeans as an exotic, mysterious land, an illusion fed by a multitude of travel reports of intrigue. But almost unknown is the literary figure who has gone beyond the impression to build his literary reputation from this very illusion—Paul Bowles, an American who has lived in Tangier for the past twenty-five years. In *Paul Bowles: The Illumination of North Africa,* Lawrence D. Stewart traces Bowles's literary career and the development of his thought from his first published poetry at age sixteen to his latest stories. Stewart structures his compelling study around the illumination motif, because light is North Africa's most compelling feature, and it has profoundly influenced Bowles's pursuits there.

"First Light," the opening chapter, depicts the young Bowles, who began his artistic career studying musical composition under Aaron Copland. He was fascinated by surrealism in music, painting, and poetry, and his work has always been concerned with the unconscious. In 1931 he met Gertrude Stein and became one of her most distinguished protégés. Having little patience with music, she directed him toward prose description and to Tangier, in both of which he was to develop his identity. He wandered in Morocco and Algeria from 1931 to 1934, then did not go back until 1947, although some of his first published stories, "Tea on the Mountain," "By the Water," and "A Distant Episode" were set in those regions and deeply rooted in his experience with the alien culture.

Stewart finds *The Sheltering Sky,* Bowles's first and most popular novel, to be the immediate result of his 1947 return to North Africa. The book is set geographically in the Algeria he had visited in the early thirties, but the events occur in the post-World War II world. Its publication in 1949 launched his career as a novelist and made him somewhat of a cult figure. In his later novels *Let It Come Down* and *The Spider's House,* Bowles has continued exploring North Africa and examining the life of the American and English expatriates there, as well as the life of the natives. Bowles's work has been most successful, Stewart shows, in its depiction of the exchange of influences

—that of people upon people, and that of the land and sky upon the travelers and natives. Although his most bizarre stories, "A Distant Episode" and "The Delicate Prey," deal with mutilation and the ultimate loss of personality, his later works, particularly "He of the Assembly" and "The Time of Friendship" affirm the opportunities to build bridges within and between cultures.

In "The Twilight Hour of the Storyteller," Stewart discusses Bowles's latest works, *A Hundred Camels in the Courtyard* and his translations of stories, novels, and reminiscences of young Moroccans. These writings reveal a profound understanding of the Moslem world, its traditional culture and its contemporary flux. Bowles's intimate knowledge of the Moslem mind has led inevitably to an exploration of the potions, herbs, and spells of North Africa, and an interest in the effect of drugs, especially cannabis in all its forms, upon man's perception of reality.

Stewart's extensive use of unpublished letters from Gertrude Stein and others, interviews with Bowles himself, and the novelist's unpublished notebook material provides fresh insights into his published works. *Paul Bowles: The Illumination of North Africa* is an excellent first in Bowles criticism.

Lawrence D. Stewart is Associate Professor of English at California State University, Northridge. He received his Ph.D. degree from Northwestern, and has worked as teacher, researcher, and music critic. Stewart is the author of *John Scott of Amwell* and *The Gershwins: Words upon Music,* and coauthor, with Edward Jablonski, of *The Gershwin Years.*

Harry T. Moore is Research Professor at Southern Illinois University, Carbondale. Among his recent books are *E. M. Forster, Twentieth-Century French Literature, Twentieth-Century German Literature,* and *Age of the Modern,* a collection of his critical analyses and miscellaneous writings. His latest books are on D. H. Lawrence and Henry James.

Crosscurrents / MODERN CRITIQUES

Harry T. Moore, *General Editor*

PAUL BOWLES
The Illumination
of North Africa

Lawrence D. Stewart

WITH A PREFACE BY

Harry T. Moore

SOUTHERN ILLINOIS UNIVERSITY PRESS
Carbondale and Edwardsville

FEFFER & SIMONS, INC.
London and Amsterdam

For *Donald K. Adams and William B. Vasels*
and the days at 629 Noyes

Library of Congress Cataloging in Publication Data

Stewart Lawrence Delbert, 1926–
    Paul Bowles: the illumination of North Africa.

    (Crosscurrents/modern critiques)
    Bibliography: p.
    1. Bowles, Paul Frederic, 1911–   —Criticism
and interpretation. 2. Africa, North in literature.
PS3552.0874Z9   818'.5'409   74–2273
ISBN 0–8093–0651–4

Contents

Now singularity that is neither crazy, sporty, faddish, or a fashion, or low class with distinction, such a singularity, I say, we have not made enough of yet so that any other one can really know it, it is as yet an unknown product with us. It takes time to make queer people, and to have others who can know it, time and a certainty of place and means. Custom, passion, and a feel for mother earth are needed to breed vital singularity in any man, and alas, how poor we are in all these three.

GERTRUDE STEIN, *The Making of Americans*

Preface

Many of us first knew Paul Bowles (born in 1910) through his music. His original compositions have been widely published and recorded, and he has written music for plays and films, as well as two operas. But he really began as a writer, as Professor Stewart shows us in this book about Bowles: when he was only sixteen, transition published one of Bowles's poems.

He virtually gave up writing during his years of composing. In Paris in 1932, he had met Gertrude Stein, who sent him to Tangier. Eventually (after the Second World War) he bought a house there and now lives either in it or on the island near Ceylon which he owns. He has written of these places and of Latin America.

He has produced four novels and several volumes of short stories, as well as an autobiography; and he has translated books by Moroccan authors. Most of his fiction justifies Dr. Stewart's subtitle, The Illumination of North Africa, for it is mostly in terms of that phrase that Paul Bowles is remarkable: the fierce colors of the terrain, of its sea, and of its sky, burn in his writing. But Bowles does more than turn out travel books or merely project atmosphere; his people have the complications found in so much modern fiction, the existential running into the absurd, with some of the characters illustrating the theme of the Westerner "going wrong" in the tropics.

American fiction has rarely treated such ideas with any profundity—there are aspects of it in Melville, however, and more than forty years ago we had Peter B. Kyne's Never the Twain Shall Meet, a ridiculous best seller with the hollow echo of Kipling in its title. We have of course had important expatriate writers, but they have usually confined themselves to Paris and London, with now and then a glimpse of Italy. But Paul Bowles—whose status is somewhat uncertain, somewhere between the negative verdict of Leslie Fiedler and the praise of Norman Mailer and Tennessee Williams—is the only serious American author who has consistently produced so much work in a remarkably exotic setting.

Time of course will show the ultimate value of his work. Now we have the first book on him, and I have found it very interesting, really engrossing, though with some inevitable disagreements, such as Professor Stewart's unadorned statement that The Great Gatsby is the best novel by the author of Tender is the Night. But such things are incidental: I am sure that other readers will find this examination of Paul Bowles and his work as compelling as I have.

HARRY T. MOORE

Southern Illinois University
February 17, 1974

Acknowledgments

I wish to thank the publishers and literary agents who have allowed me to use quotations from the following books:

Jane Bowles. *The Collected Works of Jane Bowles.* New York: Farrar, Straus & Giroux, 1966. Copyright © 1966 by Jane Bowles. Reprinted by permission of Farrar, Straus & Giroux.

Jane Bowles. *Plain Pleasures.* London: Peter Owen, 1966. © by Jane Bowles, 1946, 1949, 1957, 1966. Reprinted by permission of Peter Owen, London.

Paul Bowles. *The Delicate Prey and Other Stories.* New York: Random House, 1950. Copyright © 1945, 46, 47, 48, 49, 50 by Paul Bowles. Reprinted by permission of William Morris Agency, Inc.

Paul Bowles. *Their Heads Are Green and Their Hands Are Blue.* New York: Random House, 1963. Copyright © 1963 by Paul Bowles. Reprinted by permission of William Morris Agency, Inc. *Their Heads Are Green.* London: Peter Owen, 1963. Reprinted by permission of Peter Owen, London.

Paul Bowles. *The Hours After Noon.* London: William Heinemann, Ltd. © Copyright 1950, 1951, 1954, 1956, 1957, 1958, 1959, by Paul Bowles. Reprinted by permission of Anthony Sheil Associates Limited.

Paul Bowles. *A Hundred Camels in the Courtyard.* San Francisco: City Lights Books, 1962. Copyright © 1962 by Paul Bowles. Reprinted by permission of City Lights Books.

Paul Bowles. *Let It Come Down.* New York: Random House, 1952. London: John Lehmann, 1952. Copyright © 1952 by Paul Bowles. Reprinted by permission of William Morris Agency, Inc.; also by permission of Paul Bowles.

Paul Bowles. *Pages From Cold Point and Other Stories*. London: Peter Owen, 1968. © 1950, 1951, 1954, 1955, 1957, 1958, 1961, 1962, 1964, 1967 by Paul Bowles. Reprinted by permission of Peter Owen, London.

Paul Bowles. *The Sheltering Sky*. New York: New Directions, 1949. London: John Lehmann, 1949. Copyright 1948 by Paul Bowles. Reprinted by permission of New Directions Publishing Corporation; also by permission of Paul Bowles.

Paul Bowles. *The Spider's House*. New York: Random House, 1955. London: Macdonald and Company, 1957. Copyright © 1955 by Paul Bowles. Reprinted by permission of William Morris Agency, Inc.; also by permission of Paul Bowles.

Paul Bowles. *The Thicket of Spring*. Los Angeles: Black Sparrow Press, 1972. Copyright © 1972 by Paul Bowles. Reprinted by permission of Black Sparrow Press.

Paul Bowles. *The Time of Friendship*. New York: Holt, Rinehart and Winston, 1967. Copyright 1950, 1951, 1954 © 1955, 1957, 1958, 1961, 1962, 1964, 1967 by Paul Bowles. Reprinted by permission of Holt, Rinehart and Winston, Inc.

Paul Bowles. *Without Stopping*. New York: G. P. Putnam's Sons, 1972. London: Peter Owen, 1972. Copyright © 1972 by Paul Bowles. Reprinted by permission of G. P. Putnam's Sons from *Without Stopping* by Paul Bowles; also by permission of Peter Owen, London.

Alethea Hayter. *Opium and the Romantic Imagination*. Berkeley: University of California Press, 1968. © 1968 by Alethea Hayter. Originally published by the University of California Press; reprinted by permission of The Regents of the University of California. Reprinted by permission of Faber and Faber Ltd., London, From *Opium and the Romantic Imagination*.

Rom Landau. *Moroccan Drama*. London: Robert Hale, 1956. Reprinted by permission of Robert Hale and Company.

Henry Miller. *The Colossus of Maroussi*. New York: New Directions, 1941. London: William Heinemann, 1941. Copyright 1941 by Henry Miller. Reprinted by permission of New Directions Publishing Corporation; and also by permission of Laurence Pollinger Limited, Authors' Agents.

A Message in Code: The Diary of Richard Rumbold 1932–60.

Edited by William Plomer. London: Weidenfeld and
Nicolson, 1964. © 1964 by William Plomer. Reprinted
by permission of Weidenfeld and Nicolson.

Gertrude Stein. *Everybody's Autobiography*. New York: Random House, 1937. London: William Heinemann, 1938.
Copyright 1937, by Random House, Inc. Reprinted by
permission of Random House, Inc.; and also by permission
of David Higham Associates, Ltd., Authors' Agents.

Gertrude Stein. *Four in America*. New Haven: Yale University
Press, 1947. Copyright, 1947, by Alice B. Toklas. Reprinted by permission of Yale University Press.

Gertrude Stein. *Gertrude Stein on Picasso*. New York: Liveright,
1970. Copyright © 1970 by Liveright Publishing Corporation. Reprinted by permission of Liveright Publishing
Corporation. *Picasso*. London: B. T. Batsford, Ltd. Reprinted by permission of David Higham Associates, Ltd.,
Authors' Agents.

Gertrude Stein. *Narration*. Chicago: University of Chicago
Press, 1935. Copyright 1935 by The University of Chicago.
All rights reserved. Reprinted by permission of the Uni-
versity of Chicago Press.

Gertrude Stein. *Stanzas in Meditation*. New Haven: Yale University Press, 1956. © 1956 by Alice B. Toklas. Reprinted
by permission of Yale University Press.

Gertrude Stein. *Wars I Have Seen*. New York: Random House,
1945. London: B. T. Batsford, Ltd., 1945. Copyright 1945
by Random House, Inc. Reprinted by permission of Random House, Inc.; and also by permission of David Higham
Associates, Ltd., Authors' Agents.

Gertrude Stein, *What Are Masterpieces*. New York: Pitman,
1970. Copyright 1940, © 1970 by Gertrude Stein. Reprinted by permission of Pitman Publishing Corporation.

I wish to thank the following magazines for permission to use
quotations from their articles:

Paul Bowles. "The Challenge to Identity," *The Nation*, 26
April 1958. Reprinted by permission of *The Nation*.

Paul Bowles. "Letter from Tangier," *London Magazine* 1
(1954) and a review of Peter Mayne's *The Alleys of
Marrakesh*, in *London Magazine*. Reprinted by permission
of *London Magazine*.

Paul Bowles. "The Secret Sahara," *Holiday* 13 (1953); "The Worlds of Tangier," *Holiday* 23 (1958); "The Moslems," *Holiday* 25 (1959). © 1953, 1958, 1959, The Curtis Publishing Company. Reprinted with permission from *Holiday* Magazine.

Oliver Evans. "An Interview with Paul Bowles," *Mediterranean Review* 1 (1971). Reprinted by permission of *Mediterranean Review*.

Mohammed Mrabet. "Talking to Daniel Halpern," *Transatlantic Review* 39 (1971). Quoted by permission of Daniel Halpern.

Acknowledgment is extended to Lt. Col. Redvers Taylor and Louise Taylor for permission to publish excerpts from hitherto unpublished letters of Alice B. Toklas.

Acknowledgment is extended to Liveright Publishing Company for permission to publish excerpts from letters of Alice B. Toklas appearing in *Staying on Alone*, edited by Edward Burns.

Acknowledgment is extended to Daniel Stein, Gabrielle Stein Tyler, and Michael Stein for permission to publish excerpts from the correspondence of Gertrude Stein to Paul Bowles.

I am also most grateful to John Lehmann, Allen Ginsberg, and Lawrence Ferlinghetti for allowing me to quote from their unpublished letters to Paul Bowles, and to Gary Conklin for permission to quote from *Paul Bowles in the Land of the Jumblies*, a film by Gary Conklin. I also wish to thank the Collection of American Literature, Beinecke Rare Book and Manuscript Library, Yale University, for permission to use unpublished letters of Gertrude Stein, and the Humanities Research Center of the University of Texas at Austin for permission to use unpublished material by Paul Bowles.

Introduction

"The trouble with him," Paul Bowles once said of a friend who had dabbled in painting as well as writing, "is that he doesn't know what he is. I do: I'm a writer." That statement defines his primary interest. For has he not been a writer in the world of music too, composing operas, art songs, preludes, film-scores, and theatrical background music? Yet he would have us think first of his short stories and novels, his poetry and his journalism. In that world which he has created through language, North Africa has been his home territory. He has written a few stories about the United States, a few more (as well as one novel) about Latin America. But it is his exploration of North Africa that will give him lasting reputation. This book, therefore, attempts to cut through the multistrata of his career and see him under arbitrarily controlled conditions. (My impression remains that the non–North African work is, as he himself so frequently labels it, "diversionary," and does not alter the pattern of my findings.) The metaphor of light, which is reflected in all four chapter titles, is not meant as decoration. Light is North Africa's most compelling feature; it has been the object of, and here illuminates, all of Bowles's pursuits there.

In *The Nation* of 26 April 1958, Bowles's essay, "The Challenge to Identity," remarked how normal it was in the nineteenth century that "the desire for contact with the exotic should be satisfied vicariously through reading." But nowadays, since "anyone can go anywhere, the travel book . . . has become more subjective, more 'literary.'" "The subject-matter of the best travel books is the conflict between writer and place." "A reader can get an idea of what a place is really like only if he knows what its effects were upon someone of whose character he has some idea, of whose preferences he is aware." Bowles himself had been especially attracted to Michel Vieuchange, whose "quest was ultimately an interior one; he went in search of ecstasy, and finding only physical suffering, he was obliged to use the pages of his journal as an alembic in which to work the transformation." The writer writes to find himself; the reader reads to find the writer. "The objective presentation of his own personality . . . provides an interpretive gauge with which the reader can measure for himself." This book attempts to be the calibration of that gauge.

I have been helped in my study particularly by Paul Bowles himself, who has allowed me access to his archives and to publish selections from his unprinted manuscripts; he has also read my work-in-progress and offered invaluable criticisms. It was Andreas Brown whose foresight formed the Bowles Collection, now at the Humanities Research Center, the University of Texas at Austin; to him and his continuing attentions to that collection I am most grateful. My indebtedness to the HRC itself and to its staff is indeed considerable and acknowledged with great pleasure: to its director, Warren Roberts, to the former Librarian of the Academic Center, Mrs. Mary M. Hirth, and to John Kirkpatrick; my study could not have been made without their unfailing generosity and interest. I also offer sincere thanks to Donald Gallup, Curator of the Collection of American Literature, Beinecke Rare Book and Manuscript Library, Yale University, who has arranged for me to publish letters in the Stein Collection from Gertrude Stein and Alice Toklas; to Ira Cohen, Oliver Evans, and Jeffrey S. Miller, who have permitted me to draw freely upon their own Bowles interviews and materials; and to two of my former students, James Harstad and David A. Redman, who "talked Bowles" with me many an hour and advanced my thoughts with their reflections. I am obliged to the California State University Foundation, Northridge for a summer research grant and to Katherine Garden and Joan Lavin for help with the typescript. Nor without the support of Janet A. Kennedy, Hy Bakst, William B. Vasels and Donald K. Adams could this study have come into existence.

L. D. S.

Beverly Hills, California
26 January 1973

Abbreviations

Works by Paul Bowles

DP	*The Delicate Prey and Other Stories*
HAG	*Their Heads Are Green and Their Hands Are Blue*
HAN	*The Hours After Noon*
LICD	*Let It Come Down*
SH	*The Spider's House*
SS	*The Sheltering Sky*
TOF	*The Time of Friendship*
TOS	*The Thicket of Spring: Poems 1926–1969*
WS	*Without Stopping*
Y	*Yallah*

Other Abbreviations

HRC	Paul Bowles Collection, Humanities Research Center, The University of Texas at Austin
PB	Paul Bowles
LDS	Lawrence D. Stewart
Yale	The Gertrude Stein Collection, the Beinecke Rare Book and Manuscript Library, Yale University Library
ALS	Autograph letter signed
LS	Letter signed
TL	Typed letter, unsigned
TLS	Typed letter, signed
TS	Typescript

First Light
The Influence of Gertrude Stein, Two Early Short Stories, and "A Distant Episode"

North Africa first captivated Americans in the late eighteenth century when captivation meant literal capture, and the sailors of the young republic found themselves enslaved or ransomed by the Barbary pirates. The most noted of those to be so taken by North Africa was Captain James Riley, whose *Sufferings in Africa* went through several editions in the first half of the nineteenth century (and was read attentively by the young Abraham Lincoln). One might expect the descendants of the Barbary victims to resist the allures and avoid the snares of such a land. But where the body has been forcibly carried, there too the heart is sometimes seized. And Morocco has become, especially in this century, another outpost of the American dream, colonized by Americans in exile.

The most difficult notion to correct about Morocco is its alleged exoticism. Turn-of-the-century travel books and 1920 operettas and silent films fed that delusion. The body of literature about Morocco continues to swell. (Particularly do the English like travel books about the land as well as novels of intrigue set there.) But only the work of Paul Bowles, and perhaps that of William Burroughs, has been more than a diversion and has gained a reputation. Bowles has spent the greater portion of his life in Morocco, and his writings that deal with Barbary do so in no customary way. He has found in North Africa the ideal climate for the elucidation of character, first his own and then the native.

His work proves Montaigne's assertion that the traveler takes along, before anything else, himself. Neither Socrates nor Horace nor Dr. Johnson held out hope that travel could relieve man of that burden. Escape from self has never been Bowles's dominant interest, however. And not until well along in his career did he become the chronicler of Moroccan life (most of his travel pieces are reportage for which he has no lasting regard). Bowles has always subscribed to Gertrude Stein's notion that the artist must get away, not to lose but to recover himself.[1] (Thomas Campbell, a writer not indifferent to Algeria, reminds us: " 'Tis distance lends enchantment to the view.") Ultimately, for Bowles, that view would be of self. In North Africa's golden light, clear air, and alien culture, he and his fictive heroes work through their visions and impose upon the world a reality which otherwise, in a geographical America, could not be. Those constructs reflect not merely the American in exile but the twentieth-century American dilemma. This time, words ransom the recovery of identity.

As a seventeen-year-old freshman at the University of Virginia in the fall of 1928, Paul Bowles had already had considerable practice in constructing his private civilization. At four he had begun writing little plays and stories; and soon after, he was making up a daily newspaper for the singular circulation of himself. At six he adopted music and musical composition as a new outlet, and sometime later he tried painting. But it was words which first engaged him, and it is words which command him still.

In 1929 when any young man thought himself a free literary spirit he usually turned to Paris, where glowed the beacons of James Joyce and Gertrude Stein. Bowles's wanderlust first manifested itself when he was halfway

through his freshman year at college. The fall into rest-
lessness impelled him to Paris. As a poetry contributor
to *transition*—at sixteen, perhaps the magazine's youngest—he had read the puzzling work-in-progress of Joyce
and the equally perplexing work-as-completion of Stein.
But it was a shy young man who spent five months on
the Continent that 1929 spring and summer. "I didn't
meet one person. I didn't meet a single writer or painter
or anybody." [2] After he returned to New York that fall
he began a novel, "Without Stopping": "It was the
application of automatic writing to the general subject of
my trip to Europe, scenes put together, but not in a very
coherent fashion, I'm afraid. I was very influenced by
Finnegans Wake at that time" (Tape, LDS). "Without
stopping to think" was perhaps the allusion as well as
the process. He would later give the title of that unfinished novel to his autobiography.

After he returned to the University of Virginia in the
fall of 1929, he began work on a special expatriate
issue of *The Messenger*, the University of Richmond
magazine edited by his friend Bruce Morrissette. Bowles
thought he would solicit, among others, Gertrude Stein:
"I wonder if you could be persuaded to donate one or
two things to a small revue. . . . I cannot overem-
phasize the fact that I should like your pieces solely
because of their literary value which I feel to be im-
mense, and not to exhibit as curios (which I have
discovered, alas, to be the motive underlying the print-
ing of your work in one or two, at least, of our American
'avant-garde' mags to whose editors I have talked. They
are still unable to understand that anyone who writes
English today with any degree of mastery owes you an
inestimable debt)." [3] It was a properly deferential re-
quest to a woman who had never been gratified by sufficient publication. Miss Stein promptly sent the manuscript of "Play I" and opened a correspondence.

A year later, on 29 January 1931, Bowles sent a postcard to Miss Stein: "I am to be in Paris the first of April, and I should like intensely to see you" (Yale). The intervening months had seen the completion of his freshman year at the University of Virginia (and, as it turned out, of his college education) as well as composition studies with Aaron Copland, first in Manhattan, then at Yaddo, and then again in New York City. Thus it was as composer, and not as editor or poet, that Bowles was going abroad. He hoped to study with Nadia Boulanger and to continue his training with Copland, who also was to be on the continent.

Soon after arriving in Paris, Bowles wrote Daniel Burns, an American friend: "I called on Gertrude Stein and found her charming chumming and completely sans eccentricities, which is to say I suppose without shams. She is having me invite Aaron [Copland] to dinner the night he arrives, and is also having Bernard Faÿ whom she wants us to meet. I think it will be a great deal of fun as I like her extremely. The room she received in was huge, and had at least fifteen Picassos in it, as well as some Juan Gris pictures that I had liked for several years in reproductions." [4] Gertrude Stein herself had been astonished at the youth who appeared at her door that evening. She had expected her American correspondent (who signed himself "P. F. Bowles" or "Paul F. Bowles" or "Paul Frederic Bowles") to be in his seventies, and here he was, claiming to be twenty but looking only seventeen, and with none of the overtones of sadness she thought "Paul" conveyed. Their relationship commenced, therefore, with her rechristening him "Freddy." As she was later to tell students at the University of Chicago, "You can slowly change any one by their name changing to any other name. . . ." [5]

Gertrude Stein always had decided opinions about names and nouns, their use and power. Until she was fourteen she had not known "anybody by the name of

Paul although I always did think it was a nice name
and liked it when I saw it in a book." [6] Four years before
she met Bowles she stated about a person who is otherwise unidentified: "He was and is an, he was and is not
named otherwise than Paul. Paul is his name and Paul
is his character." [7] Later, when writing *Four in America,*
she "found it to be a fact . . . that the names that are
given, the given name or the Christian name does or do
denote character and career." And her proof seems to
have been Paul Bowles himself: "I have known a great
many Pauls. Of one of them I have even tried to change
the name, unsuccessfully. I know just what Pauls are
like even though they differ. What are they like. They
are alike that insofar as it is possible, nobody, that is
not any woman ever really loves any one of them. Now
just think of that and think how true it is. None of
them not one of them have been really loved by any
woman. They have been married and sometimes not
married, and anything can be true of them, but they
have never, dear me never, been ever loved by any
woman. That is what no Paul can say." [8] Surely that
would seem a premature judgment of a very young man.
But Gertrude Stein sensed from the beginning that Paul
Bowles was to be an intellectual loner; if there was to be
happiness in his life it must come through work. Bowles
himself has other explanations for these nominal difficulties: Gertrude Stein "had certain ideas about the aura
that goes with the name of Paul and it was too steadfast
for me." [9] "She wouldn't call me Paul because it was a
romantic name and I didn't have one ounce of romanticism in me, she said" (Tape, LDS).

Gertrude Stein had decided requirements for poetry
and poets, and she soon made it clear to Bowles that he
did not qualify. Later she explained her terms: poetry
"is a state of knowing and feeling a name"; "poetry is
essentially the discovery, the love, the passion for the

name of anything." Therefore, "nouns are poetry"—
and poetry seems inevitable: "I struggled I struggled
desperately [in *Tender Buttons*] with the recreation and
the avoidance of nouns as nouns and yet poetry being
poetry nouns are nouns." [10] Nonetheless, Bowles could
not qualify. Perhaps it was the *soi-disant* surrealist aspect
of his verse that contributed to her indifference. She
would settle, instead, for his personality and his radiant
physical beauty.

About that time she was working upon "Winning
His Way. A Narrative Poem of Poetry," which carries
on this theme of poetry and names and friendship and
a man's potentiality:

> *What is poetry. Blue clouds. In a blue sky.*
> *With many who are sitting. By.*
> *This is poetry.*
> *And friendship. What is friendship.*
> *That they mean. To be meant. Or. Sent.*
> *And they. Will. A little guess. That it.*
> *Is present. In. Their. Dress.*
> *This is May. In. Their. Stress.*
> *This is poetry and friendship and fame.*
> *And they. Will like. To know. Their. Name.*
> *With. Fame.*
> *With. Friendship.*
> *With. Poetry.*
> *With. Fame.*
> *Seriously. Meaning. Fame.*
> *This is not strange.*
> *That. It is. Seriously. Fame.*
> *Poetry. All. The same. Friendship. Made.*
> *With. Aid. Poetry. Friendship. And. Fame.* [11]

In May, Bowles and Copland went to Berlin. Copland returned to Paris after a month and Bowles took a
two-day excursion to Hanover to visit Kurt Schwitters,

who "had never heard of gertrude stein. before that. before that," he wrote delightedly to Daniel Burns (HRC). From a rainy Berlin he acknowledged to Miss Stein that "Frederic is a more sensible name in Germany anyway. It was really a trial to be forced to leave Paris when I had begun to want to remain there all the time. (But of course when I return I shall be able to play Bach)" (Yale). By that time Miss Stein and Miss Toklas had gone to Bilignin, as was their summer custom, and Miss Stein reassured the Berlin student:

> My dear Freddy,
> I am not uninterested in your poems. Bernard Faÿ has just sent them to me. I take back the harsh things I said after reading the Morada one. Alright, only its alright to learn to play Bach in poetry too, its not so easy to see how to learn but not for that any the less interesting, advice to a musician who may be a poet, who knows, Bowles, anyway if you and Copeland [sic] should pass near in going to and fro we can put you up for a few days, and we have a piano here we may even be said to have two its a nice quiet country. (HRC)

On May twentieth Bowles answered from Munich, where he was attending a music festival: "I am glad (gladder than that really) that you don't dislike all the poems as much as the first one. I was quite discouraged by the finality of: 'He's not a poet. No. He's not a poet' that evening. Things look up. The weather here is not at all pleasant. I am trying to think of a good excuse for being near enough to Belley to warrant my visiting you . . ." (Yale). But to Daniel Burns he confided, "gertrude stein writes saying come and visit. . . . my plans are not definite. i shall probably visit gertrude stain! my new name for her, in the latter part of july while copland goes to london, and then he will pick me

up there and we shall go to cannes. and that will be the
end of all" (HRC). The projected "end of all," as it
turned out, really began his literary life.

Bowles arrived in Bilignin on July 22nd. At the beginning of August, he wrote Daniel Burns:

> This section I love. Ten days I have been here, and
> each day Miss Stein has taken me on splendid drives
> through the mountains, to Aix-les-Bains, to Chambery,
> to St? Genix, to Vieux. . . . Tomorrow evening
> Aaron [Copland] arrives from Paris at Culoz, and we
> are driving up to get him. He and I will probably
> leave next Monday from Aix-les-Bains by autobus
> P. L. M. for Grenoble, where we shall spend the
> night, having visited the Grande Chartreuse en route.
> Tuesday night we shall arrive at Nice, our Mecca.
> Our Minervana. . . . I expect to finish my sonata,
> and work on several other things I have begun re-
> cently. . . .

There was a further benefit from the days in Bilignin:

> I am also getting a light on Miss Stein's own works,
> which become constantly more difficult. All my theo-
> ries on her I discover to have been utterly vagrant.
> [We hear no more about "gertrude stain!"] She has
> set me right, by much labor on her part, and now the
> fact emerges that there is nothing in her works save
> the sense. The sound, the sight, the soporific repeti-
> tions to which I had attached such great importance,
> are accidental, she insists, and the one aim of her writ-
> ing is the superlative *sense*. "What is the use of writ-
> ing," she will shout, "unless every word makes the
> utmost sense?" Naturally all that renders her "opera"
> far more difficult, and after many hours of patient read-
> ing, I discover that she is telling the truth, and that
> she is wholly correct about the entire matter. (HRC)

Another letter went into more detail: "by sense G. S. means just that. Signification. The same sort of sense one expects to find in Carlyle, or Thackeray. Of course, as she points out, it is very subtle: the sense of the motion between the sense made by various seemingly unrelated sentences" (HRC). The August letter had gloomy news about his own prospects: "all my poems are worth a large zero. That is the end of that. And unless I undergo a great metamorphosis, there will never be any more poems" (HRC). Bowles recalls her saying to him, "Now Bravig Imbs, for instance [whom Bowles had called 'one of my pet poets'], he's just a very bad poet. But you—you're not a poet at all!" (Tape, LDS). Despite these attacks, the young man recovered from his poetic despair and continued to write poems. Nor would they be the only evidence of his having his own way with automatic writing. Increasingly, however, he emphasized meaning. He would retain a composer's ear for sound and balance, but become cerebral and less trusting of his uncensored intuitions.

Meanwhile in Bilignin the "failed poet" and the literary lioness were acting out strangely engaging roles for each other.

> She'd say, "Ah, Freddie. Freddie, Freddie." She would do that all the time and I would just grin and giggle. I was playing a part. She wanted me to be this naughty little boy. She wanted me to dress in short pants which she called "Faunties." . . . I was twenty . . . but she saw me as twelve, that's the point, and that was her whole kick with me, I know. She was sort of a very loving grandmother. (Cohen interview)

Thirty years later, Alice Toklas was still remembering that summer. "Short trousers . . . Shorts! Shorts! and sneakers on his feet. And a heavenly smile of his own—he was very beautiful. . . . Aaron Copland had come to meet him there, to see him, to find out why he hadn't been working. . . . We had a good time with him. And then Gertrude took him into town in these clothes and he shocked the population." [12] Certainly there had been a physical charm to the relationship. But there remained the barrier of his poetry. And what about his music? Gertrude Stein

> wasn't particularly interested in music. She thought it was an inferior art. She once sent me a cartoon out of the *New Yorker*, I remember, two women sitting on the beach looking at a little boy digging in the sand, and one woman said to the other, "We're very disappointed in Arthur's horoscope. We thought he'd turn out to be a painter or *at least* a musician." She was very proud of that. She was always trying to put me in my place. (Cohen interview)

According to Bowles, "She had eyes, but she had no ears. She couldn't tell a tune, whether it was going forwards or backwards. . . . She had an ear for . . . assonance, dissonance, consonance. . . . But I don't think she had an ear for pitch, and I think that's the basis of liking music" (Cohen interview). When Bowles played for her one of his own compositions, "She said it was not attenuated enough. And later I played it to her and she said it was too attenuated!" (Tape, LDS). There was a quarrelsomeness to the relationship, but also a tenacity; and whether they were conversing together or writing on postcards, there was ever the tugging on a leash, as Miss Stein struggled to curtail the wandering young man. Forty years later, when Bowles wrote his autobiography, the annoyances and contentiousness of the original relationship resurfaced.[13] Yet that association permanently shaped his attitudes toward his craft; he still believes, for example, that his poetry has only minor significance.

In the autumn of 1932, when she wrote *The Auto-*

biography of Alice B. Toklas, Gertrude Stein characterized Bowles as "delightful and sensible in summer
but neither delightful nor sensible in the winter. . . .
Bowles told Gertrude Stein and it pleased her that
Copeland [*sic*] said threateningly to him when as usual
in the winter he was neither delightful nor sensible, if
you do not work now when you are twenty when you are
thirty, nobody will love you." [14] Again, perhaps it was
the matter of emotional involvement; if a young man
could not find the woman who would love and look after
him, then his work must be his guardian.

The ladies, Stein and Toklas, correctly sensed a willing
passivity in Bowles that lent itself to adult influence.
And now, in the summer of 1931, they were about to
give the young man a new sense of direction. Alice
Toklas prided herself on sitting with her back to the
view, but she had uncanny ability for putting people in
a proper setting—particularly a Spanish one. In the rue
de Fleurus salon, the men gathered around Gertrude,
and their attendants around Alice. "It was like a Moroccan room, really," remembers Bowles. "Gertrude put a
lot of space between her and Alice and thus between the
men and their wives and girl friends. . . . it was two
separate groups, generally" (Tape, LDS). Although it
had been Gertrude Stein who directed Robert Graves to
Majorca, it was Alice Toklas who had sent Hemingway
to Pamplona. (Indeed, it was also she who ignited Gertrude Stein's Spanish enthusiasm which erupted in *Four
Saints in Three Acts.*) And now she was to head this
twenty-year-old American across the Strait of Gibraltar
to Morocco.

Bowles remembers that when he was getting ready to
leave Bilignin, Miss Stein asked him where he was going.

And I said I think I'll go to Villefranche, which is
where Cocteau was, and Glenway Wescott and those
people. . . . I thought it would be nice to be in that

kind of environment. . . . And then she said "O shame on you! Anybody can go there. Why don't you go somewhere worthwhile?" But I said, "But where? I want to be where it's warm and pleasant and I want to be by the sea, and that seems like the right place." She said "Ugh!" And then Toklas, as I remember, said, "Why doesn't Fred go to Tangier?" And they both agreed that was the ideal place for me. (Tape, LDS)

If he could be delightful and sensible only in summer, then he would be sent to a winterless land. They also recognized in the youth's passivity a need for external stimulus that must not, however, be involving but curiously alienating.

Five years after she and Alice Toklas had sped Bowles on his way, Gertrude Stein explained the artist's need for alienation:

It has always been true of all who make what they make come out of what is in them and have nothing to do with what is necessarily existing outside of them it is inevitable that they have always wanted two civilizations. . . . There is no possibility of mixing up the other civilization with yourself you are you and if you are you in your own civilization you are apt to mix yourself up too much with your civilization but when it is another civilization a complete other a romantic other another that stays there where it is you in it have freedom inside yourself . . . and nothing else is a very useful thing to have happen to you. . . .

She especially sought a romantic civilization which "has no time it is neither past nor present nor future it is there because it is something with which you cannot come into contact as it exists of itself and by itself and looks as it does where it is." [15] (Years later, Bowles was still confirming her perception: "Yes, it's wonderful that here [in Morocco] there are those little—what shall I call them?—rocks in the brook that just stay there while everything else rushes by them in the water, people who just stand or sit all day while time goes by and people go by. That's the proof that life goes on, somehow, whereas in New York there isn't any proof. It's all going by, nothing going on.") [16] Gertrude Stein was apprehensive about a "completely different" civilization, such as the Orient. Such would never do, the experience there becoming not romance but adventure. Adventure is "making the distant approach nearer" (*What Are Masterpieces*, p. 62); that is the world of journalism and ordinary travel books—it has nothing to do with art.

Why would Morocco qualify as the land of romance and not of adventure? Because Gertrude Stein thought it an extension of Spain and Moorish culture and there was never any doubt that Spain was romantic and not adventurous. She invariably objected when Bowles said "Africa" and meant "Morocco." To her, Morocco was Tangier, the least Arab of its cities. Indeed, Africa would probably have been the land of adventure. But art, unlike journalism, concerns itself with the interior vision rather than the perception of externals. The strangeness of language was also essential; one could learn to communicate in his second civilization, but never like a native. Gertrude Stein could not visualize an American expatriate functioning in England, where local culture merely blurred the American experience.

When Gertrude Stein and Alice Toklas paid their first visit together to Morocco in 1912—Gertrude Stein herself had gone to Tangier briefly in 1901 and had commemorated the visit in her first novel, *Q.E.D.*—they were taking a route which many Americans before them had well marked.

Tangier is the spot we have been longing for all the time. Elsewhere we have found foreign-looking things and foreign-looking people, but always with things and people intermixed that we were familiar with before, and so the novelty of the situation lost a deal of its force. We wanted something thoroughly and uncompromisingly foreign . . . nothing any where about it to dilute its foreignness—nothing to remind us of any other people or any other land under the sun. And lo! in Tangier we have found it.

That was Mark Twain, writing in 1867 to his San Francisco audience. But his enthusiasm lasted less than thirty-six hours; "Tangier is full of interest·for one day, but after that it is a weary prison." [17] Never so for Bowles, however. His first explorations began the "romance" with North Africa, a relationship that confirmed Gertrude Stein's definition of the term, as well as Alice Toklas's perception of his personal need.

On 6 August 1931 Bowles sent a postcard from Oran to Bilignin: "We are here without believing it. The boat remains at Oran 24 hours and we arrive at Tangier the 8th" (Yale). Thus, although Morocco was his destination, Algeria became his foothold on the North African continent—a fact he would commemorate in his first novel, *The Sheltering Sky*, which begins and ends in Oran.

On 10 August he wrote Gertrude Stein again: "We are completely taken with Tangier. Houses are not plentiful, but we think we shall find a suitable one if we keep on. Piano as well. . . . The weather is blue all over and the wind blows on the beach" (Yale). By 22 August Bowles was able to tell Bilignin that "at last we are settled and the water runs from all the taps. (That has been only since this noon.) Perhaps presently we shall find someone to tune the piano so we can start using it. The weather is quite as it should be, with no variations" (Yale). But the idyl broke: the only good piano tuner was in Casablanca, and Copland could not work.

> Going into town is an event. Our estate [three kilometers from Tangier] is so secluded that it is rather easy to forget one is in Morocco, and to take the roosters' crowings and the donkeys' brayings as normal sounds. But when we are landed down at the Grand Socco, we are always pleasantly shocked. . . . Up here on the mountain there are drums that beat a lot. That worries Aaron, as he cannot get it out of his head that the Arabs are grieved about something, and are all set to go on the warpath. (Yale)

That same communique apparently also contained a story Bowles had written some time earlier and had mentioned during his Bilignin visit, for Gertrude Stein replied:

> Yes Chopin had just as much trouble with his piano in the Isles . . . so cheer up, it is the common lot. And I like your story, I like your descriptions, go on with them and send them not to the little and modern but to the older mags and see what happens, anyway, I am tired of the badness of the little ones, the others I have not seen I think are better, anyway you are not so bad in description and I always think there is a future in description, anyway love to you both. (HRC)

Bowles gratefully received the encouragement, however modest, and admitted that one critic had complained the story was the sort there's "no excuse for a grown man's having written." His musical composition seemed more successful. "The piano has not been such a complete calamity. I have managed to finish my sonata and after a few more weeks of copying its parts and the instrumental score for Miss Boulanger to read I can begin to pray nights to have it played." "The sun is always wonderful. And it always shines all day" (Yale). The climate was also extolled in a letter to Daniel Burns: "The heat here is like that of a Turkish bath. It is utterly delightful, and it is permanent. There is never any objectionable let-up that makes one so conscious of it all when it returns. Steady, hot, dry weather, with a sun that burns a white hole in the ultramarine sky, with a moon that is like the sun when it is full" (HRC). Such responsiveness to these natural and celestial phenomena played a great part in making him the kind of writer he was to be.

Early in October, Bowles and Copland moved on to Fez. Then Copland returned to Berlin, leaving his protégé behind. "Fez is full of flies and dust, and rats knock everything over on the tables at night," Bowles wrote Gertrude Stein (Yale). "It is quite dirty and *very* beautiful" (HRC). Harry Dunham, an American friend from Princeton, came down from Dresden and together they went to Marrakech and then over the High Atlas into the Zone Interdite; there the French suspected the pair of being Germans and kept them under house arrest for three days. It was Bowles's first encounter with other than a picturesque Morocco, and he began to hear of peculiar experiences which would justify his more fanciful speculations of what could happen to the lone traveler in that forbidding country. When Dunham returned to Dresden, he commissioned Bowles to bring an Arab servant ("a real savage, a real primitive" [Tape, LDS]) back to Paris for him. The Moroccan sojourn thereby ended late in November in a novel reversal of the old Moroccan custom, which had always been that the natives ransomed the foreigner.

With the exception of the venture into the Zone

Interdite, Bowles's first trip to Morocco had not detoured from the tourist's itinerary. He had visited the imperial cities, and he was ever transported by the climate of the land—its colors and temperature. (He had yet to experience the far-from-perfect weather of a Tangerine winter.) The journey even fulfilled expectations he had had, evidently, before he first met Miss Stein and Miss Toklas and they mentioned Morocco to him. Consider "Taedium Cupiditatis," which had appeared in the spring 1930 *Blues:*

the flutes of the desert are waiting
the afternoon heaves a new chill sigh
slowly of slowly a cloud unrolls
its edges blur the rim of mountains a day away

slowly of slowly the wind opens
why is the dust of this desert so fine?
a day away the sand i touch today will be a day away
    tomorrow
now that the wind's begun
bring in the rugs and fasten the flaps
smile at me once more before i forget you
sit in my company on the rug and smile
now that the wind's begun
there will be no escape from you for many hours
smile
        again

slowly of slowly the flutes of the lost desert afternoon
tremble and crumble into an evening a day away

Only the flies and the fleas and the rats had had no part in his conception of Moroccan life. But they were never to be important to him. As Bowles has reiterated in the years since 1931: "Beginning with the first day and continuing through all the years I have spent in Tangier,

I have loved the white city that sits astride its hills, looking out across the Strait of Gibraltar to the mountains of Andalucía." [18] He has looked even more the other way and always loved Mogreb-el-Acksa to the south.

Bowles returned to Paris late in November, 1931. "I see Gertrude Stein often. Her teas are often amusing. I even visit Virgil Thomson with whom she is furious. And at a vernissage the other day I met André Gide, Julian Green and Bravig Imbs. There is worse about Gide, however. My poor Arab, whom I soigneed all the way from Marrakech through Spain to here, met the scoundrel the other day in the street, and was invited to his house, where he was given silken robes, djlabas etc. Fortunately the naïf child forgot the gifts when he left. But the scandal is rampant!" (HRC).

Parisian diversions satisfied him only briefly, and within two months Bowles returned to Morocco; that second trip he spent more time in Fez, where he was locked up as a houseguest in protective custody. He caught typhoid and in June 1932, returned to Paris; but by autumn he had again returned to North Africa, moving further east and south than before, to Algiers and the Sahara and Tunisia. On 5 January 1933 he wrote Miss Stein: "I have a house down in Ghardaïa, which is too cold to live in, and so I am living at the Hôtel Transatlantique, Laghouat, Sud-Algérien. The Pères Blancs are kind and allow me to use their harmonium, at which I work all day covered by a burnous" (Yale). A month later, still exploring Algeria, he wrote her from Bou-Saada: "At the moment I am in pain, having just been thrown off the back of a crazy mare into a dry river bed. . . . I have had enough of riding beasts in the Sahara, but still I should like to see the Aurès Mts, so I am leaving this P.M. for Biskra. On the whole, camels are more fun" (Yale). Late in February he made a three-day camel trip into the desert; by March seventh he was in Kairouan, Tunisia. The train carried him to Algiers, and in April he embarked from Cadiz for the West Indies and New York. On May fifth he wrote Gertrude Stein from San Juan: "I had no desire to come to America and have no idea why I did now that I am here" (Yale).

His thoughts remained in Europe and North Africa, and in June 1934 he returned to Tangier. That fourth trip to North Africa took him yet further into southern Morocco: he crossed the High Atlas, went to Erfoud (then controlled by the Foreign Legion—mostly young Germans his own age), and inquired about going to Timbuctoo in a camel caravan. A trip to Tafilelt in mid-October produced "a mess of poems. . . . It is a magnificent country. Still murderous. The night I arrived bandits set fire to a busload of Arabs, and killed 37 of them" (HRC). By the first of November he had left Morocco, sailing this time to South America on his circuitous route to New York. After all those peregrinations through North Africa, he could scarcely have been expected to know that the junkets were over. But thirteen years would elapse before he saw the dark continent again.

In New York that 1934 spring, before the fourth North African trip, he wrote a poem, "A memory poem. It was a nostalgic poem, really, about that place and that trip, because what I'm talking about is the trip over. . . . A nostalgic evocation of my entire last three years" (Tape, LDS).

The years move outward, music from behind the trees.
In the oasis the wind roars. The palmtrunks circle.
All but the squeal of rigging, the lantern and the bells,
all but the early afternoons of distant icebergs
and accordion tangos off the Grand Banks.
All but the sadness of journeying alone,
the lostness and the sudden squalls of snow.

This afternoon we went to Amar's garden.
Finality of walls. "In Tamanar
my cousin caught a fever. You met him
two years ago, just after Ramadan.
He remembered you. He spoke once of you, last year."
And when the sun was far enough away
Amar sang a few expected songs.

The skin dries slowly, the centipedes are still asleep,
and some days the sky is sharp and dark as midnight.
At dawn the dogs howl, and again at night.
Between, each day is empty as the wind that smells of
   nothing.
The gestures are gone. Now frantic silence is here.[19]

" 'Accordion tangos off the Grand Banks' is obviously
an hermetic line, but to me it isn't, naturally. That's
part of the trip going over on the freighter." There was
no one named Amar. "I'm thinking of a particular visit
I made to a palm garden in Laghouat, outside Laghouat,
in the oasis, back in '32" (Tape, LDS). Eliot colors all
these lines, as Bowles acknowledges; but the images are
"my obsessive images. They come and go, the same ones
over and over and over, I think—I know that. . . . I
don't mind that, I don't feel that that is confining to an
author at all—necessarily, I mean. It's like a bird, I think.
Everybody really sings his song, no matter in what me-
dium, he's always singing the same song somehow"
(Tape, LDS).

Morocco would affect his work in ways he had not
foreseen; eventually it helped him master prose. In the
enforced isolation of New York he conjured up emotions that perhaps he had never known in North Africa
but which he so grounded in his evocation of that land
that the emotion and the geographical location would
thereafter be inseparable. Like a latter-day Romantic he
re-created a scene only when away from the immediacy

of its stimulus. "When the exterior life palls, the interior starts working," he wrote in December 1934. "If I moved always to new places, I should never work at all: no music, no nothing. If I were enclosed ill in a room, I should work prodigiously. . . . And it is immaterial to me which befalls me. Only not deprived of sight" (HRC). Already he apparently accepted Eluard's surrealist doctrine that the poetic function is *"donner à voir."*

In 1939 came the first of these descriptions of emotion. Five years had passed since Bowles had last seen Morocco. Then, one winter afternoon in his apartment on Brooklyn's Columbia Heights he began thinking of Tangier, of the taboos and rituals of the Arab culture, of the situation of an American novelist, living off publisher's advances, of a Moroccan experience that had not been his but pleasantly might have been. So was served up "Tea on the Mountain," his first North African short story—indeed, the first short story since he had taken an extract nine years earlier from his unfinished novel, "Without Stopping," and published it as "A White Goat's Shadow."

"Tea on the Mountain" was "a thing by itself," said Bowles. "I didn't intend to write any more. I just felt like writing it that day. I suppose it was snowing out. I just remember shutting myself in and writing this story." Then it was laid aside and forgotten. In 1949, when Bowles was gathering together stories for his first collection, *The Delicate Prey and Other Stories*, he brought it out. "It's really superficial and rather trivial, the whole story." Its one merit: "It may foreshadow things that come later in better stories" (Tape, LDS). Certainly it prefigures one of his obsessive beliefs: the need for, and the impossibility of, communication among people.

Throughout his work Bowles sets experience against

a natural background; and here he remembered Morocco by its tea ritual, the ritual of hospitality. An American woman novelist lives in the International Zone of Tangier "where life was cheap" but where she feels somewhat lonely and physically unequal to her environment. "The streets and the sky seemed brighter and stronger than she." She has formed a casual relationship with Driss, a Moslem who is Europeanized to the extent that he likes an apéritif before meals. At a café they meet some native schoolboys from the French school who wish to impress upon her that "we have Paris morals here." Two of the boys, Mjid ("serious and soft-eyed . . . eager and violent") and Ghazi (plump, Negroid and slow-witted, but son of "the high judge of the native court of the International Zone") offer to take her for a picnic at Mjid's family villa on the mountain the following day. The boys will provide a carriage, but she must bring a ham and a bottle of wine. It is thus to be a day when taboos are broken, and the novelist senses that to the bearded men in the café she is "a symbol of corruption."

But to the desperately lonely, the violating of taboos is a way to create relationships—a theme that Bowles's work reiterates. Within hours of her secret resolution *not* to go on the picnic, the woman has gathered the provisions for the outing. The carriage arrives at noon, and as they reach the edge of town Mjid presents her with a massive silver ring. "She was startled, held out her left hand." But the ring is for the index finger of her right hand. What can she give in exchange? " 'The pleasure of having a true European friend,' said Mjid gravely." But she is American, not European; that is "All the better." What she does not realize is that the boys identify her as a Nazarene, an infidel, and there- fore, they assume, available.

At the summer villa they picnic under a great olive tree. "The opening of the ham was observed in religious silence." Both ham and wine quickly disappear and then Mjid announces, in what seems a rehearsed speech, "I don't like wine, and everyone knows that ham is filthy. But I hate our severe conventions." Ghazi goes to sleep; his mother was a Senegalese slave and therefore he looks like a Negro, explains Mjid. As for himself, he pulls off his shirt and shows how white his body is. "My brother has blond hair," he announces. "It's not a question of being as good, but of being as beautiful." Mjid finds the novelist beautiful because she has blue eyes. "But even some of us have blue eyes. In any case, you are *magnificent!*"

"Suddenly she was conscious of the silence of the afternoon. Far in the distance she heard the forlorn crow of a cock. It made her feel that the sun would soon set, that all creation was on the brink of a great and final sunset. She abandoned herself to sadness, which crept over her like a chill." They return to the villa for tea, but her sense of alienation is dominant. "The idea of such a picnic had so completely coincided with some unconscious desire she had harbored for many years. To be free, out-of-doors, with some young man she did not know—*could* not know—that was probably the important part of the dream. For if she could not know him, he could not know her." This situation is hopeless. "It should have been a man, not a boy, that's all," she says to herself. But Bowles indicates that had it been a man, had the two parties belonged to the same generation, she would not have come.

Mjid sees his sexual ploy has failed, and he says despairingly that she is crazy. So he tells her of his life, of a twelve-year-old girl "like the sun, soft, beautiful, lovely," with whom he makes love all day long. Idyllic as those Moroccan hours may be, Mjid also has his dream: "Perhaps some day I shall go to America, and then you can invite me to your house for tea. Each year we'll come back to Morocco and see our friends and bring back cinema stars and presents from New York." The day has concluded with "a faint but clear voice singing." It is the *muezzin*, calling to prayer. It always makes her sad, she says. "Because you're not of the faith," answers Mjid. They return to the hotel. A long awaited cable has finally come, calling her to Paris. Mjid asks her to be sure and write. They part, and she sits in the "cramped little salon" waiting for dinner and "looking at old copies of *L'Illustration*." Already her thoughts have abandoned Morocco for Europe.

Tea has been a Moroccan ritual since the seventeenth century. "The variety of tea and the variety of mint are both, according to the Moroccans, of prime importance." [20] The quality of the water is also material, and it is this ingredient that helps structure "Tea on the Mountain." As they approached the mountain Mjid pointed out a distant village "where all the people are mad. . . . It's the water they drink." Later, as they walk together after the picnic, they are given "some foul-smelling water in an earthen jug." When the novelist speculates about its potability, Mjid exclaims "When you're offered something to drink, even if it's poison, you should drink it and thank the man who offers it." He "seized the jug from the ground between them, and taking it to the edge of the cliff, flung it down with elegant anger." Later, the water for their tea is brought from the well and is presumably pure. Throughout the story there are allusions to the sea, always visible in the distance; the last glimpse of it is implied by the lighthouse, flashing across the almost-black bay. In all civilizations, water is life; the quality of the one determines the quality of the other. Especially is this true in a poor and semidesert country like Morocco.

But westerners have needs too, and living in Morocco can satisfy some. What sort of woman is the novelist?

Nameless, alone, dressed in slacks, knowing only rudimentary Arabic, living first out of town on the mountain in a house with a bad well, and then later in a poor hotel in town, always passive, yet bringing action into her life by placing herself in the mainstream of activity. We are told nothing of her talent; she seems to live on borrowed money and borrowed hopes. Perhaps she is latently a lesbian, for her interest in Mjid's twelve-year-old girl friend (unseen but vividly spoken of) far surpasses interest in the boy himself. Although there is the hint of danger in her excursion with the boys, she can take advantage of the law of hospitality in this land of rigid social structures. Even though, as a gentile woman, alone and available, she must likely to the Moroccans be a whore, her being given food and drink and shelter makes her an equal under the protective eyes of Allah.

The tea ceremony—like hospitality itself, which is to unite men in peace and understanding—here shelters perversion. The religious dietary laws are broken, and the woman is far older than the boys; she likes Morocco only for the cheapness of the land and the cheap availability of a qualified but delicious terror. We have the prelude to the sexual act, but timidity and indifference interfere. It is the hunt without the kill. Tea becomes the confederation not of those who wish to give themselves to bonds of love and friendship; it is the confederation of those who wish to get. Since terror is an essential ingredient to her pleasure, she flaunts her money and her solitude, pretending to be an easy victim. But this courting of danger is only the courting of vulgarity. As she draws money from her publisher for work that is promised but not delivered, so she extracts emotions from the boys, using Mjid as she has used Driss earlier, "putting him off without losing his friendship."

"Tea on the Mountain" is not an effective story; it oversimplifies the conflict between worlds. But in its themes it predicts what is to follow: the attraction of the unknown, the loneliness of the contemplative mind in a culture that is never clearly understood, the desire for—and the impossibility of attaining—true friendship across cultures. Everyone wants to know himself and to know his image, man. The act of writing is the act of projection: writing to an audience, building a bridge, fusing experience. But bridges collapse, fusions separate, and man ends as he began, alone. In the first of his Moroccan stories Bowles took his protagonist toward a glimpse of this awareness and then released her from the burden of self-knowledge by letting her escape to Paris. The weakness of the story is its assumption that Morocco can be put on and removed as casually as its native djellaba. Later, Bowles will make dramatically convincing the idea that once North Africa has been perceived, there is never an escape from perception. The existence of this story proves that.

After "Tea on the Mountain," another five or six years elapsed before Bowles tried a second short story, "The Scorpion." Both it and "By the Water," a North African story written in 1945, are, according to Bowles, "surrealistic," rooted in private memories. For example, Bowles says he once knew a man in Fez who resembled the fantastic Lazrag of "By the Water." "He could only reach up to the rungs of a chair. He could reach about as far as the seat of the chair I was sitting in, with these flippers that came out of his shoulder, like a seal" (Tape, LDS). The *hammam* too mirrored a memory: "The pool is, again, from another place. The pool I'm thinking of is not really underground—it's in a sort of cave. It no longer exists, it's been destroyed by the Moroccan government" (Tape, LDS). For Bowles the story is "a synthesis of memories"; but that rearrangement of observed phenomena does not explain its intention, structure, and peculiar effect.

Bowles's use of the term *surrealistic* is somewhat personal. He has applied it to his poetry, particularly the more hermetic, where images succeed one another in a logic that is not known to the poet's conscious mind. Such poetry, according to Bowles, either works or does not. And though elements are consciously identifiable, they cannot be explicated in any sensible way that would account for an insistence that pressed them into use. "You understand whatever you understand" (Tape, LDS). Surrealism in fiction obviates planning, for planning "would require knowing what you are going to write before you write it—which I don't. I sort of open the door and plunge into this unknown world—and then suddenly the door of the ending appears, and I go out again. But what's happened while I was inside, I don't really know" (Tape, LDS). The first door is discovered by the inexplicable urge to write. Sometimes the urge comes accompanied by a detonating phrase that sets off the artistic unconscious; sometimes the urge produces an image. Bowles once called "By the Water" "an experiment in automatic writing. . . . I sat down with no previous idea in my head, wrote the thing without 'knowing' what I was writing, and at a certain point stopped, probably because I was physically tired, and called that the end" (HRC). Emphasizing the unreality of such reality, he omits descriptive details of person and of place. Amar lives "in the city" and goes "to visit a neighboring city where his father had once told him some cousins lived." Amar's city is the "better and larger" of the two; but that is all we are told. Only when there is an essential physical characteristic, such as Lazrag's physical deformity, are we given the appearance of a character.

The plot: Young Amar, "being alone in the world, decided it was time to visit . . . some cousins." He arrives in their city late at night and, in searching for a place to stay, enters a strange *hammam* which seems a secret club rather than a public bathhouse. He undresses and is led to the pool by a dirty and ragged little boy, Brahim, who "looked rather more like a midget than a child." Brahim tells Amar about the diabolic power of Lazrag, the owner, who can turn a man into a bird. Suddenly the deformed Lazrag appears and challenges Amar's presence in the grotto. Amar kicks the head of the dwarfish creature, who rolls into the pool and sinks. The bathers immediately rush after Amar, but he escapes to the center of town, where he is found by Brahim who promises to find him shelter. But no place will receive them, and they walk out of town. Amar "was pleased that the boy wanted to stay with him, but he did not think it fitting to say so." After an hour a truck gives them a ride on top, and the child is delighted: "Lazrag has found us and changed us both into birds. . . . No one will ever know us again." They arrive at the seashore and Amar walks into the breaking waves; suddenly an enormous crab crawls toward him. Frightened, he leaps backward and hits his head on a rock. Just as the crab reaches Amar's feet, the boy screams *Lazrag!* and the crab scuds away. Lying in the rushing water, Amar "felt the boy trembling in his effort to hold his head above the waves, and he heard him saying many times over: 'I saved you, Amar.' "

Beneath the superficial level of dreams and logical fallacy, there is a tighter world of psychological validity; and it is there that the story relates to themes which run throughout Bowles's work. If in "Tea on the Mountain" we see the conflict between Western civilization and the French–civilized Arab culture of North Africa, we here examine that essential conflict within a culture itself. Amar is characterized only by his loneliness in the late winter. "Spring was on the way, to confuse the heart and melt the snow." Like his northern compatriots, who in April long to go on pilgrimages, so in this false spring Amar too wishes to join himself to the world in bonds of familial love. He travels to a strange town—a colder town, in the mountains, where the snow is still deep in the streets—to see people he has never known but who allegedly are relatives.

He is drawn to the *hammam* by "a few languid notes being strummed on an oud." (In Bowles's world, music frequently traps man into expressing his primitive instincts.) Once inside the bathhouse, Amar finds that the boy, Brahim, seems mainly interested in money. When he asks Amar if he has much, Amar tells him he will be paid in the morning when the traveler is awakened. The boy disappears, only to reappear as the guide and comforter after Amar has eluded his pursuers. We do not know the basis for the attraction between them, though Bowles implies that the boy runs after Amar. The reason for love is not explained in the surrealistic dream, where events follow each other and seemingly thereby construct a linkage of cause and effect. Certainly the boy believes himself demonstrably the antidote to magic, for his shouting *Lazrag!* has turned the crab from his prey. This assurance of power makes Brahim believe Amar will now be in his debt. The exchange of services, the giving of something, the gratifying of a desire—this will be a theme in the later works. Too there will be developed, as a leitmotif, the difference between generations and its pernicious effect. In the world of Paul Bowles the young either do in, or assume mastery over, their elders, in the ultimate inversion of natural order. Thus, for Bowles, the surreal world is where wishes become fulfilled and people triumph to the degree that they willingly express themselves and their psychological drives. The triumph seldom accords to social law and the more conventional arrangement between sexes and between generations.

Bowles's most famous attempt to give surreality a persuasive realism is undoubtedly "A Distant Episode." This widely anthologized story was written around 1945 and published in the *Partisan Review* (Jan./Feb. 1947). The story is of violation and horror; a simple professor, a linguist who surveys "variations on Moghrebi" (the lingua franca of the Sahara, "basically Arabic with some Berber words" [Tape, LDS]), travels south where he is captured by a roving band of natives and has his tongue cut out. Dressed by them in a costume made from "the bottoms of tin cans strung together," he becomes a pet and diversion, cavorting and gesticulating wildly to entertain the tribesmen and their women. Again Bowles has expressed the impossibility of cross-cultural bridge building. The Professor (who is nameless, merely a label) is even more lonely than the woman novelist or Amar of the earlier stories; and in his emotional isolation he turns to a climate of violence where, perhaps, liveliness can give quality to life.

> The experiences of a man who lives alone and in silence are both vaguer and more penetrating than those of people in society; his thoughts are heavier, more odd, and touched always with melancholy. Images and observations which could easily be disposed of by a glance, a smile, an exchange of opinion, will occupy him unbearably, sink deep into the silence, become full of meaning, become life, adventure, emotion. Loneliness ripens the eccentric, the daringly and estrangingly beautiful, the poetic. But loneliness also ripens the perverse, the disproportionate, the absurd, and the illicit.[21]

We do not know that Bowles was influenced by Thomas Mann's "Death in Venice," where the above observation was made; but the motivations of the two protagonists, the Professor and Gustav von Aschenbach, occasionally parallel. Each man is impulsively driven to cultivate his own destruction, no matter how enriching and meaningful that "destruction" may seem to him.

Bowles's account begins with the September sunsets "at their reddest" and ends with "the lunar chill . . . growing in the air." Once again the context of nature and temperature reinforces a state of mind. And as the novelist in "Tea on the Mountain" had scant understanding of others, so this linguistics professor does not know how to communicate. He has, after four years, learned Moghrebi, but his only personal contact has been with Hassan Ramani, a man whom he had known for three days ten years earlier and "who had written him several times during the first year after his visit, if never since." The Professor now finds out that Hassan Ramani is "deceased." His dreaded experience begins not, however, with that discovery but with his expressed desire for "those little boxes made from camel udders," the sort of container that is sold in the far south by the Reguibat. Certainly he has heard of that tribe: "The Reguiba is a cloud across the face of the sun," and "When the Reguiba appears the righteous man turns away." But his interest is not in the meaning of words and maxims. Nor is he concerned with the source or significance of the camel udder boxes. To him they are merely souvenirs without memories. Evidently he does not know that they are traditionally used by women for keeping kohl, the native cosmetic. But those who do not react appropriately to the world and its rituals are, according to Bowles, undone by what they disregard. So the Professor who lives by language loses his tongue; and he who would collect the box of a woman's make-up does himself become an ornament and a diversion in a primitive culture.

In "Tea on the Mountain" the woman novelist "looked at . . . [Mjid] tenderly, and decided that his face was probably the most intense and beautiful she had ever seen. She murmured a word without quite knowing what it was." The word is *Incredible*. Later, after Mjid had given her his address, he wrote "Incredible" beneath it: he knew that whatever the strange word meant, it had incapsulated him for her. The reader infers, however, that she has not really seen the boy. Only for a moment has he become a thing of beauty, the accessible male she had previously avoided. The woman novelist is unwilling to believe in life as involvement, and she rejects beauty, the enticement to sexual fusion; instead, she turns emotions into rhetoric which distorts and conceals. "Incredible," written in such hope by Mjid, underscores ironically the impossibility on her part of any profound perception and belief.

In "A Distant Episode," that same word, *incredible*, crystalizes a similar self-deceit. The Professor is taken by the *qaouaji* to the edge of an abyss where a path leads downward. Though terrified, the Professor has already surrendered himself to the experience of the unknown. His lips move "automatically. They were saying: 'Is this a situation or a predicament? This is ridiculous.' " He lay on the ground and looked at the moon. "It was almost like looking straight at the sun. If he shifted his gaze a little at a time, he could make a string of weaker moons across the sky. 'Incredible,' he whispered." He gets to his feet and makes his way down the path into destruction, where the incredible is made credible, the ultracivilized is reduced to the most primitive. "It occurred to him that he ought to ask himself why he was doing this irrational thing, but he was intelligent enough to know that since he was doing it, it was not so important to probe for explanations at that moment." The expert who has mastered language to unlock the secrets of reality, is led into a suprarational experience which suggests darker drama within the id. In some mad fashion, the working-out of the story recalls Emerson's *Nature*: "Every man's condition is a solution in hieroglyphic to those inquiries he would put."

Bowles himself does not account for the story's existence by literary parallels.

> *That* I happened to write because of having a dental appointment. I think I was going to have an extraction. . . . I was on my way up and I took an IRT subway train from where I was, dreading the experience, but fortunately I had a little notebook with me, so I thought I would provide a counter-irritant, fight fire with fire, so I began writing a story. . . . And I had perhaps a page, or a page and a half, written by the time I got to Columbus Circle, and then I went on to the dentist's office, which was on 57th Street, and went on writing even more feverishly because the moment of truth was approaching and I do not like to have teeth extracted.[22]

For writers, it is not a singular reaction. "Waiting to have a tooth extracted one often gets involved in the plan of a new book; one fairly seethes with ideas," says Henry Miller. "Then comes the torture, the book is expunged from the consciousness; days pass in which nothing more brilliant is accomplished than sticking the tongue in a little cavity of the gum which seems enormous. Finally that too is forgotten and one is at work again and perhaps the new book is begun, but not as it was feverishly planned back in the cauterized waiting-room."[23]

Bowles's story has even more complicated origins, however, curiously recalling the sights of childhood when his father was a dentist and his family had a laundress named Sylvie Ann. The writing of the story extracted a memory from 1933:

I found an amusing passage in one of the letters [to my mother], dated March 17, 1933: "One afternoon I saw a great tall woman in front of our hotel. She looked like Sylvie Ann, and was just as black. But whenever she moved there was a jangling like a junk wagon, for she was covered from head to foot with the tops and bottoms of tin cans which she had carefully cut out. Hundreds of the bright discs hung from wires she had strung about her cadaver-like body. The largest ones she had made into a girdle, which she constantly removed, examined, and put on again, talking all the while. Then she would bend down to great clanking and have a little conversation with a mound of dust she would scrape together. Then she would straighten herself, amid more music, and threaten to pull down the sky. Then she would sadden once more, and remove her belt, looking at it intently." (This is clearly the origin of the Professor's costume in EPISODE.) [24]

He still retains the story's detonating detail: a small box made from a camel udder. In 1934, Bowles was visiting Erfoud in the south of Morocco and was trying to arrange a caravan for Timbuctoo. "They told me about this old man—I've forgotten his name—who had been there for many years, and he said, 'Yes, but the trip will take you over a year.' So I didn't do it, naturally. I wasn't that far gone that I was going to take a whole year out" (Tape, LDS). The old Frenchman gave Bowles a small camel-udder box. It had a painted top (the design is now almost invisible) and had been made by the Tuareg. Even in 1934 Bowles knew that that kind of box had never been Moroccan but came from the legendary regions to the south.

The story begins with the geographical setting and the presentiment of blood and horror. The town of Aïn

Tadouirt is imaginary, but the name of the murderous tribe is real. "In the first version," said Bowles, "the bad tribe are the Chaamba.[25] And then when I went back to Morocco and began moving around I decided to change that to the Reguibat." The Chaamba are in central Algeria, the Reguibat in Mauretania; but it is not essential that the reader understand this distinction. "I think it's clear, it's implicit. I could have called them— *anything*" (Tape, LDS). The story's shock comes solely from the experience itself. "Shock is a *sine qua non* to the story. You don't teach a thing like that unless you are able, in some way, to make the reader understand what the situation would be like to *him*. And that involves shock." Shock can be therapy for the author; it can also be an indulgence. "Insofar as he wants only to shock, he's a victim. No, I can see that a lot of my stories . . . had a therapeutic purpose behind them when I wrote them. For me personally. I needed to clarify an issue for myself, and the only way of doing it was to create a fake psychodrama in which I could be everybody" (Evans interview).

Like the Professor, he was working to bridge the transition from entity to identity, from involvement to the detached vision.[26] For the Professor, his sale to a man in Fogara is the loss of entity; and the loss of entity is a return to pain. "It operated in a kind of delirium, because he had begun to enter into consciousness again." And that consciousness inevitably brings him to "an access of terror," deprived as he is of the novelist's ability to channel safely the drives that otherwise destroy one. Bowles's achievement in the story convinced him he could make his own myths believable by "adopting the point of view of the primitive mind" and calling that private mythology "fiction" (WS, pp. 261–62).

"A Distant Episode" bores into all levels of Bowles's

life and thought; it is ironic that so effective a probing brought forth a story that has sharply curtailed his audience. In 1952, Harvey Breit put several questions to Bowles and asked for a definition of decadence. (The assumption behind the question suggests the lingering power of "A Distant Episode.") Bowles wrote back: "I should think in art and literature nothing is decadent but incompetence and commercialism. If I stress the various facets of unhappiness, it is because I believe unhappiness should be studied very carefully; this is certainly no time for anyone to pretend to be happy, or to put his unhappiness away in the dark. (And anyone who is not unhappy now must be a monster, a saint or an idiot.) You must watch your universe as it cracks above your head." [27] In an undated journal he has written, "In an extreme situation, man becomes situation. Tongue-cutting merely an intensifying of general situation today" (HRC). Not even those most disturbed by "A Distant Episode" can deny there is a fissure in the universe. And through that crack had come the first light to fall upon a literary landscape that Bowles was making uniquely his.

2

The Cold and Brilliant Morning
"Pages from Cold Point" and
The Sheltering Sky

In the spring of 1947 Bowles, like Abou Ben Adhem, awoke one day from a dream of such peculiar and lingering vividness that he found his life transformed. Bowles has never disregarded omens: "Dreams do clarify your life completely . . . they tell you much more than anything else could possibly tell you, about what you really want and how much you're willing to sacrifice to have it and what it entails, you know, to help you decide and cut everything else out. Only a dream can tell you that, it seems to me" (Tape, LDS).[1] Thus he awoke to a vision of Tangier and to thoughts that now, after thirteen years away, he must return to North Africa. He inquired about freighters and a livelihood; and by July 1st, when he embarked from New York aboard the *M.S. Ferncape*, bound for Casablanca, he was able to take with him not only the continuing eagerness for Morocco but a contract signed with Doubleday for a first novel, a project which would help finance the expedition and also give it shape.

Among the miscellaneous papers carried on board was a typewritten two-and-a-half page "start" for something (he was not certain exactly what), transcribed from a manuscript he had written some months earlier on a briefer journey when he had taken the train to Mt. Kisco, New York for a weekend with Samuel Barber and

Gian Carlo Menotti at their home, Capricorn. Perhaps
that destination had stimulated him, for Capricorn had
a reputation for literary inspiration. Bowles thinks there
was an additional cause: "Being in motion always ex-
cites me, apparently, and I began scribbling." It is true
of him as it was to be of Port in *The Sheltering Sky*:
"Whenever he was en route from one place to another,
he was able to look at his life with a little more objec-
tivity than usual. It was often on trips that he thought
most clearly, and made the decisions that he could not
reach when he was stationary" [SS, p. 105]. Now upon
the water, again in motion and—more significant for
his creative impulse—in an environment "that is not a
continuation of anything," Bowles went to his cabin
and looked for that earlier "start." "I took it out and
suddenly felt that I would like to write a story. I didn't
know exactly what was going to happen, of course"
(Tape, LDS).

What happened was "Pages from Cold Point," "a
long story about a hedonist; it had been vaguely trying to
get born for six months, ever since my visit to Jamaica"
(WS, p. 276). Though the tale would seem to be a thing
apart, we can better understand Bowles's North African
writings by first examining it and the conclusions to
which it brought him. For much seems to have come
from this story. It first appeared in *Wake* magazine
sometime during 1949. That same year it was included
in *New Directions 11*; and in 1950 it was republished in
The Delicate Prey and Other Stories.[2] Norman Mailer
singled out "*Pages from Cold Point*, a seduction of a
father by a son" as "one of the best short stories ever
written by anyone,"[3] and the story is generally considered "characteristic Bowles," i.e., sexually shocking.
It is characteristic in other ways as well: the protagonist
is again a college professor who gets himself into a
bizarre situation and acts out atavistic fantasies; to that
extent the story parallels "A Distant Episode."

"Pages from Cold Point" is the reflective journal of Norton, a bored college professor who, through the recent death of his wife, has become financially independent. He abandons teaching and takes his sixteen-year-old son, Racky, to a remote Caribbean island "beyond the reach of prying eyes and malicious tongues" to be his only companion at Cold Point, a splendidly isolated house on the cliffs above the sea. The boy, who shared his father's indifference to school, flowers in his new freedom and bursts into a homosexual life with the natives, men and boys in the village eight miles away. Awareness of this is brought home to Norton by the local constable who whispers "like an eager conspirator": "Keep him home . . . Or send him away to school, if he is your son. But make him stay out of these towns." Neither solution will satisfy Racky who must now pry loose the stranglingly affectionate hold his father has on him.

Before they had left the States the boy had overheard a conversation between his father and his uncle and had correctly deduced that they had had, in their youth, an overt sexual relationship. The uncle has never resolved his own attitude toward the adolescent experience and, transferring his guilt to Norton, thinks him an unfit parent. When Racky senses that his own homosexuality has become known to his father and has put him even further under Norton's control, he silently puts himself —passive but naked—into his father's bed; and the lives of the father and the son become dominated by these nightly filial submissions. The pleasure is Norton's and not his son's, however. Within weeks Racky suggests that his uncle be invited to the island for a visit; he can stay in "my room. . . . It's empty." Racky has well remembered Uncle Charlie's threat: "if there's any trouble with the boy I'll know who's to blame." Norton suddenly sees where all is leading; so he himself proposes the freedom that Racky wants. He takes the boy to Havana, sets him up in an apartment, buys him a convertible, and assigns him the larger portion of the mother's estate. Then Norton returns to Cold Point, far from that dreaded civilization which presently encroaches no further than fifty miles away, cross island. He will still think occasionally of the atomic bomb that might demolish his island life; but he pays no mind to that immediately partial, and eventually total, loss of income that must end the days at Cold Point.

Despite the somewhat unusual sexual material in the story, Bowles himself has seldom shown much literary interest in the sexual act—thought, for him, always being more compelling than any deed. The boy's seduction of the father is but means to a greater end; and bringing about an action is, for Racky (as for most Bowles characters), merely gaining awareness of one's fundamental nature. It is discovering what Gertrude Stein, in her own analysis of personality, called one's "bottom nature" and then arranging a context so that it can best manifest itself. Playing upon the father's suppressed homosexuality and bringing it into the open releases for Racky the door to his personal freedom.

"Pages from Cold Point" is presumably a journal Norton kept on the island; this method of presentation makes the story bewildering but also psychologically engrossing. It is the prose presentation, by a main participant in the action, of that action as he performs it—without awareness of an overall pattern until it has revealed itself. And it confirms what Bowles once noted in a notebook: "What you do is nearer to what you are than what you think is" (HRC, "Decorative Material"). Not the least problem in deciphering the action is both the journal's deliberate self-deceptions and its unconscious suppressions. Only the reader can provide the compensatory parallax that will bring the subject into focus and perspective. Originally Bowles dated the entries Nov. 6 to Jan. 17 (no year); but he erased the dates and put asterisks between entries, still emphasizing that this is indeed a journal of a crisis. We must not forget that the account is rendered by a man whose university career has been "an utter farce (since I believe no reason inducing a man to 'teach' can possibly be a valid one)." The journal's audience, therefore, is only the compiler. He may disdain the academic life and its published self-justifications, but he still lives totally by and in reflection. Norton will seldom be able to discuss any significant problem or situation with his son, and he can give expression to the unvoiced thought only in his diary.

Bowles himself has never encouraged this approach to reality. "Even one word alone expresses a thought," he wrote a correspondent in 1961, "and thoughts can only be reflections of what goes on outside" (HRC). Norton's journal is not merely an accounting for the immediate past, nor is its writing an existential act divorced from a temporal continuum. Instead, suppressing, emphasizing, reordering, it creates a present moment with remembered materials. "I can never believe in the gratuitous, isolated fact," Norton put in his journal. The appetites of yesterday now feed the structure of ideas and will produce what both Norton and Bowles consider "happiness."

"Pages from Cold Point" builds skillfully on parallels and the return of images "from days I [Norton] dislike to recall." Racky now looks the way his Uncle Charles did when the brothers, Charles and Norton, were having their adolescent sexual relationship. And though Charles has "thick, red face and hands" and a "back-slapping, joviality" as well as "fathomless hypocritical prudery," he once, like Racky, possessed "the lithe body, the smooth skin, the animal energy and grace." For Norton to sleep with Racky, therefore, is for him to sleep with more than one person. To the degree that the child is partially the father's creation and re-embodiment, it is a narcissistic act. More significantly, the act denies time and regains for Norton that initial sexual experience with his admired older brother before there was guilt and then hatred. The past is recaptured by making love to it: physically with the child, rhetorically with the journal. Much of the story's psychological interest stems from this balancing off old accounts. We play again with the ambiguities of the child as father to the man.

Whatever the widower Norton's relationship had been with his wife, Hope, we cannot disregard the puzzling fact that she exists here unmourned—either by father or son; she is only a financial source of present life. The death of Hope released Norton from his scheduled experience and allowed him to act out his fancies and his fantasies: "that week [which settled her estate and his affairs] was the first time since childhood that I had managed to recapture the feeling of there being a content in existence." The death of hope is basic to the perception of Nothing, which in turn can produce an existential "happiness."

Norton keeps his journal because he can project an image that stirs him—not necessarily to action but to acceptance. At crucial moments he looks in the mirror for his regeneration: "I saw my eyes trying to give their reflected brothers a little courage." Norton thinks of events themselves only after he has first considered the process that has brought them to his attention. And this aspect of Norton's character (which Bowles presumably considers the plight of the "intellectual") [4] gave the story its conception. From that "start" which Bowles scribbled on the train trip to Mt. Kisco, only the final three paragraphs remain in the story as printed today. The original opening reveals Bowles's first view of Norton as a man in a world that is neither chaotic nor structured but the moment-by-moment projection of a man with "incomplete powers of perception" ("one [who] believes what one must"):

> I think the concept of chaos is just as false (and by false I mean man-made) as, let us say, the concepts of perfection or objective truth. Undoubtedly a state of absolute irrelevancy is unattainable, appearances to the contrary. But then, as I say, all absolutes are only results of the working of the human mind with its inevitably incomplete powers of perception. I should not like it to be generally thought that I am so victimized by the circumstances of my life as to have become a misanthrope, and yet the fact remains that my immediate feeling for everything directly relating to humanity is one of profound pity. And of course pity is a kind of loathing. I sit here on the terrace directly above the pounding of the waves against the cliffs, and I am conscious that only the proximity of an element so infinitely more powerful than man (how I hate the word "man") makes it possible for me to continue my round of eating, sleeping, defecating and receiving consciousness. (I hate the word "man," yes. It seems sometimes that in any other language it is more acceptable. But of course that is an absurdity!)

"Eating, sleeping, defecating and receiving consciousness"—these alone concern Norton; and he pays scant heed to the nature of Camus's "absurdity" which hovers in the background of the story. But his journal chronicles only the receiving of consciousness—the other processes will be a concern in *The Sheltering Sky*.[5] "Receiving consciousness" is not to be equated with learning the truth; for Norton's account concludes not with the statement that he now knows what he is but that he is "perfectly happy here in reality." (Bowles himself has said the story ends happily, for "Happy is the man who thinks he's happy" [Tape, LDS].) [6] Thus Norton refuses to watch the sky crack over his head, or the ground give way beneath him. The reader knows that Racky will return to claim the rest of his mother's fortune, that that great house "like a large glass boat filled with orchids and lilies" will founder on these rocks it presently rides above, and that Norton will have to return to his detested academic life. But Norton speculates about none of this in his journal. The journal is the reflective act by which he lives and, in a novel reversal of Newton's third law, the reaction that gives whatever action there is to his life.

Indeed, the journal ventures even to translate personal experience into legend, as it calls the sexual idyl with Racky "the recompense I had unconsciously but firmly expected, in return for having been held so closely in the grip of existence all these years." The details of that evening of the seduction "have taken on the color of legend." Perhaps Norton saw himself as Laius and Racky as his Oedipus. Homosexuality is as basic to the legend as to this reality. "I felt the fascination of complete helplessness that comes when one is suddenly a conscious on-looker at the shaping of one's fate," wrote this later father. But Norton cannot create a legend; he can only relive it and draw pleasure in that recognition.

Gertrude Stein's distinction between identity and entity—between literary detachment and aesthetic fusion—can help illuminate Norton's discovery that "Destiny, when one perceives it clearly from very near, has no qualities at all. The recognition of it and the consciousness of the vision's clarity leave no room on the mind's horizon." Such fusion with, and detachment from, *dolce far niente* may partly be owed to the tropical locale. Most likely it is fulfillment of a certain kind of expatriate temperament. Expatriates are not merely those who shift their geographical location. Like Fitzgerald's rich, they are peculiarly different from ordinary folk: they possess early and what they possess is neither lost nor augmented—something like a magical dry cell that, while it never gives off much life, is strangely immune from a total loss of power. Isolation may have "resultant fears and hostilities; [but] they are the fabrics of life, not the pattern woven into the fabrics" (HRC, ms. opening of "Pages," later deleted).

Norton occupies his insular days in ways unchronicled, except for those previously enumerated natural processes, plus swimming, sun-bathing, and occasional cycling. Like that marvelous house, perfectly attended to by silent but cheerful servants, nature too reveals herself only as idyllic: crickets chirp, water runs, the air blows; everything works naturally and without undue attention. The only communication with the outside world (other than the mail which irritably summons Norton cross-island on occasion) is the day-old newspaper. No mention of a radio, no mention of creature comforts that might divert the bored ear or eye. Some books to read, but no one other than Racky to talk to, no phonograph to play, no companions for cards or drinking or for any communal pleasure. No mention of sex (other than the experience with Racky), of the need to create, to build, to affirm the continuum of life. Because, of course, what Cold Point most offers, and what Norton most values, is Nothingness. Had he not told his academic associates, " 'Nothing,' when I was asked, as invariably I was, what I intended to do" and considered that answer "the greatest pleasure I felt in all this"?

When Norman Mailer praised Bowles's story he did not extend that praise to the novels that followed: "his characters are without life, and one does not feel that the author ever lived with them.[7] He does not love them and certainly he does not hate them—he is as bored with his characters as they are bored with each other, and this boredom, the breath of Bowles's work, is not the boredom of the world raised to the cool relations of art, but rather is a miasma from the author" (Mailer, p. 468). Strength of plot exempted "Pages from Cold Point" from Mailer's criticism. But did Mailer not perceive that while boredom is not the effect of the story, certainly it is the story's focus?[8] When Norton's goal to achieve Nothingness is threatened, he carefully removes the menace: so he casually gets rid of the house-servant, Peter, who had become a conscious center for Racky's attentions. And when Racky reveals himself as a blackmailing homosexual, Norton arranges for him an active life—but far away. All that Norton fears is uncontrollable interference with the balance of nature, the atomic bomb that might demolish his island paradise. Gratuitous acts exist, for him, only on a cosmic level; therefore in time all will pass, including himself. But for the moment, by staying quiet as death, he thinks he has deceived destiny: "I do not wish anything at all." The imitation of death, this handsomely embalmed life, is for him the denial that death exists and threatens.

When Flaubert wrote Louise Colet, 16 January 1852, "What seems to me beautiful, and what I would like to achieve is a book about nothing," he carefully defined his intention as "a book with no external links, which would stand by itself by the internal force of its style, as the earth, without being supported, remains in the air, a book which had almost no subject, or at least where the subject was almost invisible, if that were possible. The most beautiful works are those which have least material."[9] The notion has since become almost a commonplace; certainly its accuracy was proved by Gertrude Stein, who had begun her career by translating

Flaubert's *Trois Contes*. Flaubert's reshuffling of Aristotelean parts of a tragedy gave primacy to thought and diction. Flaubert pursued his *"mot juste,"* and Bowles too has always believed that only diction creates: a sentence is predicted by what precedes it and must never be the conscious manipulation of an author, adjusting his rhetoric to fulfill his plan. Thus "boredom" is never "nothingness" for Bowles; nor is nothingness itself ever vacuity.

The rhetoric in "Pages from Cold Point" does more than sustain a narrative: it gave Bowles title and concept for his first novel. After he had finished typing the story —or at least the "start" for it—he penciled in its title: "The Sheltering Rocks." Though that adjective itself does not occur in the story, the image logically defines the experience. For that rocky cove below the house shelters Norton in his nudity and in his delusion: he lies there in the sun, thinking that time can be stopped, yet listening to the movement of the tide, believing that the barracuda and sharks are beyond the reef and that the natives dare not trespass by land. But it is there, in that cove, that the idyl breaks when the village constable intrudes to tell him the truth about Racky. Nature had deceived him: "how powerful they are, all those physical elements that go to make up its atmosphere: the sea and wind—sounds . . . the brilliancy of the water, sky and sun, the bright colors and strong odors of the flowers. . . ." The regained Paradise is again to be lost in "unusually low tide"; and the rocks have been delusive shelter. Small wonder that in the original version of the story, Bowles had named Racky "Rocky." That version had concerned the sheltering of Rocky, and Rocky as delusive shelter for Norton. But there was no protection in that relationship, any more than there had been invulnerability in the natural shouldering of sea and cliffs and the house itself.

When named "The Sheltering Rocks," the story ended with Norton sentimentally remembering an island expression, "Tears don't show in the rain." Originally his involvement with Rocky was not to have been so easily forgotten, even though he did add "Figurative tears, of course." For at no time had it ever been other than Cold Point, the traditional temperature for reason and the dispassionate intellect. Happiness is thought, for Norton. And emotion itself becomes a nonsensual state of mind in that cold and brilliant light.

Bowles erased "The Sheltering Rocks" as title, penciled in the matter-of-fact label, changed the boy's name, and cancelled his sentimental conclusion. But the problems raised in the story were not so easily solved or dismissed. Nature as barrier and shelter, as the mask of meaningful reality in a cosmic drama—that perception became the "start" for his first and finest novel, The Sheltering Sky.

"Pages from Cold Point" perhaps did not so much create new ideas and attitudes for Bowles as rescue unconscious notions which had lain trapped within him. By the time he disembarked in North Africa all sorts of thoughts were uppermost in his awareness: there was the escape from American civilization into an isolated and natural world which both comforts and destroys; there was the attempt to see reality by private vision only, an absence of plan balanced with an almost religious faith in protective improvisation. Finally there had emerged a fear of man that verged on misanthropy and encouraged the deliberate violation of taboos and the working out of private ritual that is its own salvation. All these had been churned up on that crossing. (Three years later, in a notebook marked "Accounts," Bowles wrote out a translation of man as The Complicated Animal: "It puts love on one pedestal. Death on another. On the highest of all it puts whatever it does not know and cannot know, and that which has not even any meaning. It adds an extra world to this one. We are by nature condemned to live in the imaginary and the unfinishable" [HRC].)

Bowles began *The Sheltering Sky* almost immediately and spent a year in the writing, writing it all over Morocco (Tangier and Fez) and Algeria (Taghit, Béni Abbès, Adrar, and Timimoun). But it was begun and ended in Fez. Occasionally he interrupted the work for a diversionary short story (such as "Señor Ong and Señor Ha") set in another part of the world. But because he seldom found it comfortable to write of his fictive setting if he were physically within it, he never confused the two Algerias: "the one of fifteen years back, which was a completely different region of the country, and the one in which I was living. Everything in the book came out of the first Algeria, the remembered one, of course, with the exception precisely of the details I arbitrarily listed as I wandered around the oases" (TLS, PB to LDS, 26 Nov. 1972). As for those small ingredients which came from immediate perception: "I would reinforce each such scene with details reported from life during the day of writing, regardless of whether the resulting juxtaposition was apposite or not" (WS, p. 278). The technique had also been Gertrude Stein's, though Bowles was not conscious of its being so. In writing "Melanctha," she had woven into her story "poignant incidents" noticed on her daily walks to Picasso's studio (*Autobiography of Alice B. Toklas*, p. 60), even though her story was set in a remembered Baltimore.

The novel's plot: Three New Yorkers decide in the "Atomic Age" (presumably 1947) to go to North Africa, "this distant and unconnected part of the world" (SS, p. 105). Port and Kit Moresby and their friend, Tunner, land in Oran and slowly move south through a fantasy landscape of towns and oases with invented names [10] into the reality of the Sahara; separated first by chance or whim, they are separated ultimately by death and self-willed abandonment. Yet there is scant change in their characters—merely the confirmation and fulfillment of the natures they had brought with them: the intelligence of Port in pursuit of romance, the emotions of Kit in the involvement with adventure.

An undated manuscript fragment sums up Bowles's attitude that the novel dramatizes: "The only effort worth making is the one it takes to learn the geography of one's own nature. But there is seldom enough energy even for that. One must accept one's own limitations as one accepts life and death, pain and pleasure. Only then can these natural defects be utilized to their fullest extent. Resistance cripples. Life is I want, which in turn is beautiful and good. The less complex the desires, the more likely they are of attainment. The act of dying must be longed for as the ultimate attainment. Any philosophical or religious system which can instill this longing is justified, but not if doing so involves any sort of rejection. By striving with every facet of the imagination to conceive of chaos, one manages only to explore a little more carefully the terrain of order. To develop one's sensual characteristics, no matter how subtly, leaves one at the mercy of the physical world and its increasingly destructive onslaught. It takes an exceedingly insensitive person today to be able to continue being an artist" (HRC).

Port Moresby, the dominant interest for two-thirds of the novel, seeks the silence and solitude which alone make possible the liberation of the unconscious. Civilization is, after all, suppression: the imposition upon the individual of some structured view of the world. The characteristic of the Sahara is its silence, its extremes of temperature, its sky: there, where the niceties of life are nonexistent and where survival is itself the challenge, only man can bloom. Two years before Bowles wrote *The Sheltering Sky*, Gertrude Stein had published her own credo about man's dependence upon his environment: "After all anybody is as their land and air is. Anybody is as the sky is low or high. Anybody is as there is wind or no wind there. That is what makes a people, makes their kind of looks, their kind of thinking, their subtlety and their stupidity, and their eating and their drinking and their language." [11]

Bowles's attitude toward the desert occasionally reminds us of Camus's. Themes of this novel also parallel the conclusions of Jung: "The deeper we penetrated into the Sahara, the more time slowed down for me; it even threatened to move backward. The shimmering heat waves rising up contributed a good deal to my dreamy state, and when we reached the first palms and dwellings of the oasis, it seemed to me that everything here was exactly the way it should be and the way it had always been." Jung had found that among desert people, "consciousness takes care of their orientation in space and transmits impressions from outside, and it is also stirred by inner impulses and affects. But it is not given to reflection; the ego has almost no autonomy. The situation is not so different with the European; but we are, after all, somewhat more complicated. At any rate the European possesses a certain measure of will and directed intention. What we lack is intensity of life." [12]

A hundred years before Bowles saw North Africa, Delacroix was urging: "come to Barbary and there you will see those natural qualities that are always disguised in our countries, and you'll feel moreover the rare and precious influence of the sun, which gives intense life to everything." [13] The sun that dominates consciousness— that was North Africa's essential contribution. When Gide had first found Oscar Wilde in Algeria, Wilde

confessed, "I want to adore only the sun. Have you
noticed that the sun detests thought? It drives it ever
back, into the shadows." [14] Bowles himself, in making
notes about Brion Gysin's paintings, stressed that "The
S. [Sahara] is the place of the great lie, where nothing is
true save that light makes it so. (a pitiless & capricious
light). Shadow can have more reality than rock, the sky
can be more solid than the earth beneath" (HRC).

Bowles conceived a three-part structure for *The Sheltering Sky*, both in plot and character, and paralleled
experiences to contrast and illuminate. Originally Bowles
thought of the book as one long narrative and used
asterisks to moderate the flow—the technique tried out
in "Pages from Cold Point." Eventually he turned the
marked divisions into chapters and the three parts into
books: Book One: "Tea in the Sahara"; Book Two: "The
Earth's Sharp Edge" (originally "The Passport"); Book
Three: "The Sky" (once tentatively labeled "The Bed").
Epigraphs were supplied for each. (Book Two had
carried, temporarily, an additional one: Camus's "An
ignorant spirit; that is, a solitary one," perhaps deleted
because the existential references were not always to
seem appropriate or to be encouraged.) [15] The titular
revisions tone down the sensational aspects of the plot,
for Bowles was never to be happy with descriptions that
stressed the melodramatic in his story.[16] Triangulation
also plots the three characters' journey into awareness
and compasses their path across desert and under the
sky. Other individuals—natives and intellectual nomads
—will cross their trail; but while that same sun will shine
on all, it burns into clarity and reduction only Kit and
Port Moresby and seldom more than silhouettes their
uncomprehending shadow, Tunner.

On several occasions Bowles has recollected his in-
tentions in *The Sheltering Sky*. The 1952 letter to
Harvey Breit compared the novel to music, although

Bowles conceded that he had "felt extremely circum-
scribed in music. It seemed to me there were a great
many things I wanted to say that were too precise to
express in musical terms." But he recognized the inevitable correlation: "In 'The Sheltering Sky' I did
think of the three parts as separate 'movements' but I
can see that was an error. A novel is not a symphony or
a sonata. If it's anything that can be compared to music,
it's a melody." That is, its strength must be in its plot.
Nearly twenty years later he reviewed his conception of
his first book: "I didn't plan *The Sheltering Sky* at all.
I knew it was going to take place in the desert, and that
it was going to be basically the story of the professor in
'A Distant Episode.' It was an autobiographical novel,
a novel of memory, that is. . . . *The Sheltering Sky*
was . . . a working out of the professor's story. . . . In
my mind it was the same story retold; it described the
same process in other terms. . . . I wanted to tell . . .
the story of what the desert can do to us. That was all.
The desert is the protagonist." But the desert has no
priority to the sky. "It's all one: they're both the same,
part of nature." Nature is not antagonistic, she is merely
indifferent. "Not caring. Unaware. And if you use the
word God in place of nature, then I think you get even
closer to it" (Evans interview).

Without Stopping gives us to understand that the
novel's title and certain formal details had consciously
emerged on a Fifth Avenue bus ride, largely from a
recollection of childhood: "Before the First World War
there had been a popular song called 'Down Among the
Sheltering Palms'; a record of it was at the Boat House
in Glenora, and upon my arrival there each summer
from the age of four onward, I had sought it out and
played it before any of the others. It was not the
banal melody which fascinated me, but the strange
word 'sheltering.' What did the palm trees shelter

people from, and how sure could they be of such protection? . . . The book was going to take place in the
Sahara, where there was only the sky, and so it would
be *The Sheltering Sky*. This time at least I did not have
to lie awake nights searching for the right title. In
essence the tale would be similar to 'A Distant Episode'
. . . and it would write itself, I felt certain, once I had
established the characters and spilled them out onto the
North African scene. By the time I got up into midtown
I had made all the most important decisions about the
novel" (WS, p. 275).

There is also one other fragment of evidence. In
November 1950, Bowles inscribed a copy of the novel
for a collector who had asked for an "interesting" remark: "The only 'interesting' thing I can think of to
say is that *all* the characters in the book exist, some
with the same names used here." [17]

No artist can be expected to remember all the forma-
tive details of his work. Indeed, to the degree that he is
an artist and coalesces into an "entity" with his work,
no detached memory is possible. What rough sketches
for *The Sheltering Sky* may have existed have not been
preserved, but three typescripts remain. Each is unique,
but all are appreciably close to the published book. [18] It
is the novel's title that poses a problem. The precise
moment that "The Sheltering Rocks" was penciled in as
title to what eventually became "Pages from Cold
Point" cannot be determined. Perhaps "The Sheltering
Rocks" was a title that Bowles had given only the "start"
which he carried aboard ship—given it sometime after
the "start" itself had been typed (for the title has been
penciled in). The title could have been assigned before
Bowles had thought of writing a novel; therefore, when
he titled the novel on his Fifth Avenue bus ride he
could regard the title of the "start" as discarded. No
matter when the transfer was made, however, the

evidence persuades us to believe that the "protective" concept had first come into Bowles's consciousness in connection with what became the story.

First, let us accept Bowles's statements and consider the parallels between the novel and "A Distant Episode"; and then let us re-examine the relationship to "Pages from Cold Point." We should not disregard the coincidence that the central figures of both stories are rather dim-witted or self-deceived college professors. The Professor in "A Distant Episode" has begun his adventure symbolically, in pursuit of "little boxes made from camel udders." Since his interest in them is expressed impromptu, we assume that he is a novice collector and that his inquiries are merely the lonely man's ploy to strike up conversation and gain attention. But his mistake leads inevitably to his dehumanization, as the collector finds himself to be the trophy. Chapter 5 of *The Sheltering Sky* is a somewhat parallel experience. Port is not looking for camel boxes; indeed, he thinks he is looking for "nothing" when a native lures him to the outskirts of town with the promise of a wild animal girl. When Port descends into the native encampment in the valley beneath Oran, the ambiance is the same as in the story. But the Professor is an immediate victim, caught up in a circumstance he cannot comprehend: he knows he is going into danger and is not at all sure why he yet goes on. Port, on the contrary, has consciously created the circumstance in which he places himself; and he successfully escapes—admittedly, a close escape—from entrapment. (Later, Port would enunciate the relationship between rational and instinctive reaction: "He could make the right gesture, or the wrong one, but he could not know beforehand which was which. Experience had taught him that reason could not be counted on in such situations. There was always an extra element, mysterious and not quite within reach, that one had not reckoned with. One had to know, not deduce. And he did not have the knowledge" [SS, p. 130].)

In revising his typescript, Bowles altered the conclusion of the episode in chapter 5 more than any other event in the novel. Originally he had focused upon the struggle between Port and his pursuers: the cry of the native girl had aroused the men in the neighboring tent; and as Port rushed out, he collided with one of them. "Swiftly Port hit him. He felt the bridge of a nose under his fist. The man screamed now: 'Ayayayay!' " Men were coming from the two sides to cut him off from the staircase, but Port scrambled away, got to the top of the stairs where he seized

> a boulder he could not lift, he did lift it, and hurled it with unerring aim down the staircase against them. Instead of turning to run, he stood there, heaving and sagging, and watched. It had hit the first one in the middle of the body, knocking him over backward against the oncoming two behind. Then it had bounded into the legs of the second. He had gone over with a cry, and lay quietly below, the rock somewhere near him. "So many days of hanging onto life, and now nothing," thought Port as he saw it happen. The third man was holding the unconscious first one, trying to keep him from going over, and calling loudly to others below. There was the sound of feet hurrying up the iron steps at the bottom. Port breathed deeply and began to run along the parapet. (HRC: this was intended for SS, p. 41)

It was the Professor's experience again, this time with the Professor fighting back and triumphant—even killing one of his pursuers. But Bowles did not publish the account. A revision shifted the theme of the novel as it had begun to take shape in this early episode and eliminated the reality of the danger: no man rushed in from a neighboring tent and was hit by Port. Admittedly there was "a man coming from one side to cut him off from the staircase," but he was the only pursuer. (And perhaps even his existence was unintentional: Bowles marked his typescript to read "he thought he saw a man coming from one side, to cut him off from the staircase," but inexplicably that revision did not get into print.) Port expected to be caught, and when he reached the top of the parapet "he turned, and seizing a boulder he could not lift, he did lift it, and hurled it down the staircase. Then he breathed deeply and began to run along the parapet." That boulder had been hurled at no apparent target. In the original typescript "the loud sound of his own heart . . . did not keep him from hearing the excited voices of his pursuers below in the road"; but now an inserted phrase ("did not keep him from thinking he heard the excited voices . . .") merely dramatized Port's anxiety. Whatever the demons that pursue him and drive him south into the emptiness of the Sahara, they are never to be cinematic ruffians whom he can slay with bravado and elude with impunity.

The Sheltering Sky's plotted similarity to "A Distant Episode" is initially misleading, for the episode that began the Professor's transformation is merely a diversionary excursion for Port and has no permanent effect upon him and no consequences for the novel. Only in the final section of the novel will experiences again parallel the Professor's; but there they will be the adventures of Kit which re-echo conclusions arrived at in "A Distant Episode." The situation of "Pages from Cold Point," on the other hand, affected the development of *The Sheltering Sky* from the beginning.

In "Pages from Cold Point" the dual concerns of Norton had coupled, dramatically but unclearly, within the narrator. In the first draft of that story Bowles had concentrated upon the father-son sexual relationship:

Norton revealed himself to be an emotionally involved but guilty and fearful adult who accepted his final isolation with relief mixed with shame and sadness. In revision, Bowles blurred Norton's physical yearnings for his son; and by reordering the philosophical speculation, which had begun as the self-deception of the father-seducer, made it psychologically persuasive. The reader can never comfortably accommodate what Norton says to what Norton does; and thus he is denied the aesthetic response created by, for example, Mann's "Death in Venice." *The Sheltering Sky* separates the two aspects of Norton—the sexual and the philosophical—to build a character from each. In their interplay they would occasionally recall the themes and structural problems of "Pages from Cold Point." But Bowles could now handle his ideas more easily and subordinate the sexual to the philosophical, as he had so evidently wished to do in the revision of his short story.

A recurrent belief that amounts almost to a fixation in Bowles's world is that the relationship between parent and child—or between an adult and a youth—is invariably destructive. "Pages from Cold Point" recorded this in an overtly homosexual context. In *The Sheltering Sky* we will see it as the incestuous relationship between mother and son.[19] The theme was already a set one in Bowles's fiction before he encountered, unexpectedly, the real-life illustration of it. When he started his novel, he ran into "a highly implausible couple, a mother and son whose behavior was strange enough to interest me. In an unlikely series of coincidences spread over a period of two or three months, we found ourselves meeting in hotel lobbies, first in Fez, then up in Tangier, after that in Algeciras, and finally in Córdoba, after which they went on their way. By this time they were firmly implanted in the narrative of my book as subsidiary characters. Their inclusion now seems unfortunate, not because I used them, but because they turned out to be caricatures" (WS, p. 277).[20] Those encounters may have given Bowles specific details of behavior and appearance (though those physical descriptions and case histories were considerably changed in revision); but, as we have seen, the situation had already been there at Cold Point.

In the earliest version of the novel Eric Lyle was a "Teutonic-looking youth, somewhat on the chinless side, and with a starved blond moustache," "shiny blond hair," and a face "pink and blotchy." Revision made Eric into a "heavy-looking youth with a formless face which was saved from complete non-existence by an undefined brown beard" (SS, p. 53); that "full, white face" (SS, p. 263) was "suffused and puffy" (SS, p. 63). In the first version the family had been Canadian: Eric, born in 1925, is a few months short of twenty-one when the story takes place. Though Tunner may dismiss him as a "spoiled sissy brat grown up" (SS, p. 258), Kit instantly senses his duplicity. She had seen him as a "young Henriot . . . the one who pulled sea-gulls to pieces, and finally did it to his wife too." The revised galley compared him, instead, to "young Vacher . . . the one who wandered across France slicing children into pieces" (SS, p. 54)—a revision that effectively stressed the theme of child molestation which is central to the Lyles' relationship.

Though in the first version Mrs. Lyle gossiped about her son's homosexuality, flatly telling Port that Eric had gotten his disease from "Some filthy swine of an Arab woman. Or man" (intended for SS, p. 90: the latter phrase was deleted in revision), and though Kit herself had labeled Eric "probably a screaming fairy into the bargain. He certainly looks like one" (intended for SS, p. 65: those remarks too, were suppressed), Eric is to be more than merely an overt homosexual. He devours

Port with his eyes and tends to read every remark "as if he placed very little importance on the words that were said, and was trying instead to read between the lines of the conversation, to discover what the other really meant" (SS, p. 259). Neither Port nor Tunner is much interested in analyzing the young man; only Kit, who detests him, solves his mystery. She who has seen the Lyles' passports can confirm that they are indeed mother and son; she also senses that Eric hates the sexual submission he must make to his mother.[21] Like Racky, Eric is trapped—but trapped by greed and weakness; for if he is weaker than Racky, he has also a stronger antagonist than Norton. Mrs. Lyle may indeed approach caricature, but she is an effective monster.

In the first typescript Mrs. Lyle had appeared as a "small, bustling, pink-faced woman, with white hair and a doll's blue eyes." Born in Montreal, she had become "a commercial artist" and had spent, with her son, "eight African years . . . moving haphazardly between the Cape Colony and Tangier" (intended for SS, p. 59). Revision changed her into a "large, sallow-skinned woman, her hair fiery with henna" (SS, p. 53). Her passport now classifies her as a "journalist" born in Melbourne (SS, p. 96); and the eight African years were parceled out to three in India (where an elder son had died) and five in Africa. Mrs. Lyle "wrote travel books and illustrated them with her own photographs" (SS, p. 59). Tunner, who always saw simplistically, dismisses her as "a sour, fat, gabby female" (SS, p. 258). But Port perceives that behind the apparent paranoia and anti-semitism is "the loneliest woman he had ever seen." His awareness does not endow her with sympathy, however. For her, "the dispute . . . [is] the natural mode of talking" (SS, p. 74) and she betrays a deviousness as deep as her son's: "her deportment was a roundabout means of communicating an idea she dared not express directly" (SS, p. 91). She is so unsympathetic, so caricatured with her glassy black eyes, her gleaming make-up, and her high voice ranting about trivialities that there is little interest in her deeper mystery. And when the Lyles finally disappear, they are forgotten.

When Bowles first introduced Eric into the novel, however, he evidently envisioned a greater use for the young man. After all, it was Port who initiated their relationship; he found in Eric not a sexual deviate but a potential existentialist. "There was no question of its being an interesting or an uninteresting conversation as far as the young man was concerned, since what he was saying was merely a device useful to the moment at hand, and the subject was a convenient fiction to be elaborated upon according to the exigencies of the situation" (intended for SS, p. 59). That sentence and that interest in Eric were deleted in manuscript. Not cut, however, were the occasional parallels drawn between Port and this mock villain, whether they are reading maps or being strangely attracted by physical violence. There is even a moment, at the height of Port's desert rapture with Kit, that he turns to her—not as to a wife but as to a middle-aged mother; for he is adolescent even as is Eric. We may know less of Eric's motivations than we do of Racky's; and only Racky triumphs in that battle between generations. But Eric is more than a device to steal passports and help move the principals across the desert of lost identity. Faintly as we may perceive the outlines of his mind and character, we can glimpse subtle parallels and counterpoint to the more engrossing and central relationship between the Moresbys, husband and wife.

Aristotle's assertion that only the plot—the choice and arrangement of incidents—can establish character and demonstrate its quality is well tested in this novel. Partly because of the foreboding world that Bowles creates, partly because of the mysterious personages who cross those visionary landscapes, we feel compelled to *understand* the characters of Port and Kit. For to the degree that *The Sheltering Sky* has meaning, it rests on our comprehension of those two products of our civilization: so like us, the readers, and yet so memorably unique and alone. In his original typescripts, Bowles gave little space or thought to the physical description of the Moresbys. Only in the galleys did he add such a detail about Kit as: "Small, with blonde hair and an olive complexion, she was saved from prettiness by the intensity of her gaze. Once one had seen her eyes, the rest of the face grew vague, and when one tried to recall her image afterwards, only the piercing, questioning violence of the wide eyes remained" (SS, p. 15). Even when he was compelled to see Kit up close, Bowles still wished to blur impressions.

Eventually the plot will complete the characterization of Kit as she moves into what Gertrude Stein called "adventure." But Bowles allows comprehension of Port only by returning us to the philosophical speculations of Norton: action becomes "romance"—a process of the mind, turning inwardly upon itself: one's "bottom nature" will be tracked down not through the inevitable repetitions of speech and behavior but in the recesses of the imaginative memory. Therefore in revising his novel, Bowles consistently suppressed those incidents which, in the more conventional dramatic work, would define the protagonist.[22]

The novel opens with Port at a moment of almost-apprehended awareness: "He awoke, opened his eyes." It is from the sleeping moments within our lives that Bowles brings back into waking consciousness glimpses and clues of who and what we are. "Since early childhood it had been a fantasy of mine to dream a thing in such detail that it would be possible to bring it across the frontier intact—the next best thing to being able to hang onto all those fistfuls of banknotes that must always remain behind when the eyes open" (WS, p. 165).[23] Port opens his eyes in the Oran hotel with "the certitude of an infinite sadness at the core of his consciousness, but the sadness was reassuring, because it alone was familiar" (SS, p. 11). Port is not a Byronic hero—he lacks galvanic energy and elements antithetically mixed —but he will prove Byron's belief that there is a vitality in despair. The action of the novel works itself out from the precept. "The mere certitude of being alive" is, for Port, "not sufficient" (SS, p. 11). As he will later confess to his wife, "We've never managed, either one of us, to get all the way into life" (SS, p. 101).

Each will try in different ways to get there. A principle of Port's had always been: "Whenever the thread of his consciousness had unwound too far and got tangled, a little solitude could wind it quickly back" (SS, p. 131). He will discover that his journey into life "had been one strict, undeviating course inland to the desert." There, "very nearly at the center" (SS, p. 198) and celebrating his birthday—"the one I've been waiting for" (SS, p. 213)—he will encounter the "famous silence of the Sahara" (SS, p. 202)—the epitome of sought isolation, of "solitude and the proximity to infinite things" (SS, p. 100).[24]

Little in Port's appearance or public behavior creates the philosophical complexity that the omniscient narrator asserts he has. Physically he is "young"—probably in his mid-thirties—and thin, "with a slightly wry, distraught face" (SS, p. 13). He is occasionally petulant; his actions are frequently the improvised responses of one whose nature is not merely passive but obdurate. "My world's not humanity's world. It's the world as *I* see it" (SS, p. 95), he will proclaim, when cornered. The world does not return the regard with such indifference; it kills him

with typhoid when he (who from student days in Paris
and Madrid had made forays into North Africa and
should have remembered well its hazards) indifferently
avoids the shots that would have preserved him. Or are
we to regard it as more than indifference—another aspect
of the intellectual self-abuse that separates him from his
wife? From the beginning of the journey, he was "unable to break out of the cage into which he had shut
himself, the cage he had built long ago to save himself
from love" (SS, p. 100).

Money has not troubled him, but Port has still not
entirely escaped the Puritan ethic of justification by
work. He calls himself a writer—though we see no evidence of production. "As long as he was living his life,
he could not write about it" (SS, pp. 199–200) says
Bowles. In Algeria, however, Port temporarily deceives
himself with the attractiveness of "A journal, filled in
each evening with the day's thoughts, carefully seasoned
with local color, in which the absolute truth of the
theorem he would set forth in the beginning—namely,
that the difference between something and nothing is
nothing—should be clearly and calmly demonstrated"
(SS, p. 199). If such were true, why bother even to keep
a journal—that grid imposed upon the chaos of life?
Because, as we discover, Port thinks he can believe in
reality only if it is verbally conceptual. Again we are
reminded of Norton and that other journal which
celebrated nothingness but which gave life to a protagonist.

A mystical perception of the unity in nothingness is
Port's justification for passivity: if "the quantity of
pleasure, the degree of suffering . . . comes out even
it's only because the final sum is zero" (SS, p. 167).
That perception—and the self-willed adherence to it—
gives him cerebral form for us and makes him more than
merely the somewhat haggard and furtive adolescent

seen by those who do not perceive his quality. Not for him conventional pursuits, not for him the travelogue desert. "Glacial deadness" is "the core of his being; he had built the being around it" (SS, pp. 140–41). And thus the Nothing of the Sahara is not decorative or diversionary—it reinforces his self-perception. Like that earlier crusader, Richard the Lion-Hearted, he feels an instinctive "unsureness about the *no* and the *yes* . . . the inevitable attitude one had if one tried to consider the value of that life" (SS, p. 74). But balance is maintained precariously, and even self-asserted nothingness requires a healthy power in the assertor. When Port sinks into his typhoid raptures, " 'No, no, no, no, no, no, no,' he said. It was all he had the strength to say. But even if he had been able to say more, still he would have said only: 'No, no, no, no' " (SS, pp. 217–18).

Hence, the desert and the sky are never neutralities: "the sky here's very strange," he tells Kit. "I often have the sensation when I look at it that it's a solid thing up there, protecting us from what's behind" (SS, p. 101). The fusion, however much desired, is never easily attained. "The rocks and the sky were everywhere, ready to absolve him, but as always he carried the obstacle within him. He would have said that as he looked at them, the rocks and the sky ceased being themselves, that in the act of passing into his consciousness, they became impure" (SS, p. 168). Ultimately, near death in his typhoid delirium, he sees that "the thin sky stretched across to protect him. Slowly the split would occur, the sky draw back, and he would see what he never had doubted lay behind advance upon him with the speed of a million winds" (SS, p. 233). "Frail and tottering, the sky will be rent asunder on that day," says the Koran, "and the angels will stand on all its sides with eight of them carrying the throne of Allah above their heads. On that day you shall be set before Him, and all your secrets shall be brought to light." [25] But not for Port a Mohammedan paradise beyond that sky. The Koran affirms that Allah "holds the sky from falling down: this it shall not do except by His own will. Compassionate is Allah, and merciful to men" (Koran, p. 393). Port's sky, however, has been sustained only by his will, his belief in its power as symbol. And he, who had paid no attention to the needs of his body—nor even to the sexual and physiological needs of his wife, so immersed has he been in his own meditations—is ultimately destroyed by disease, as metaphysics becomes only metabolism.

> His cry went on through the final image: the spots of raw bright blood on the earth. Blood on excrement. The supreme moment, high above the desert, when the two elements, blood and excrement, long kept apart, merge. A black star appears, a point of darkness in the night sky's clarity. Point of darkness and gateway to repose. Reach out, pierce the fine fabric of the sheltering sky, take repose. (SS, p. 235)

Port's sky is not Shelley's dome of many-colored glass; it is more like MacLeish's circus tent—the membrane that separates us from "nothing, nothing, nothing—nothing at all." Perhaps it can be defined in no other way: no thing, no common denominator of human experience, the *res* of the world. Void, vacuity, emptiness—they all suggest a negative, but limited, experience, the experience this side of the membrane, under the circus tent, under the sheltering sky. Here within limits we are permitted the formal, albeit arbitrary, gesture—the exertion and expression of self in the existential act. But beyond the membrane, where there is no thing, there is perhaps no act possible. That is the ultimate horror, that is the ultimate comfort.

Bowles solved the problem of the sky's meaning and

devised a means of dramatizing Port's death by turning to drugs that would psychologically alter, temporarily, the chemical balance of his own mind. It was an important moment in the working out of his aesthetic; its success in this novel began the concern with cannabis that would be both theme and practice in much of his subsequent writings.

Bowles first tried marijuana in Curaçao, in December 1932, but wrote his friend Daniel Burns that "I have since decided [it] is not quite healthy to use" (HRC). Alethea Hayter, a student of the effects of hashish, has written, "It is only in cultivated reflective melancholy minds that hashish can produce its full effect, the excessive development of the poetic spirit." Baudelaire's *Les Paradis Artificiels* is the most famous document of those effects, "how time and space stretched to infinity; and how, finally, they passed into the 'kief,' the sensation of absolute god-like superiority and happiness, a perfect self-satisfaction and complacency which could even admire its own remorse." [26] Bowles himself ate majoun to elicit the needed images: "Very consciously I had always avoided writing about death because I saw it as a difficult subject to treat with anything approaching the proper style; it seemed reasonable, therefore, to hand the job over to the subconscious. It is certain that the *majoun* provided a solution totally unlike whatever I should have found without it" (WS, p. 279).

There had been a mad tergiversation in Port's fever, a demonic yo-yoing of his psyche. When he had first lost his energy ("It takes energy to invest life with meaning") his will could no longer keep the essence of things from retreating "on all sides to beyond the horizon, as if impelled by a sinister centrifugal force." Nor could he then face "the intense sky, too blue to be real, above his head" (SS, p. 160). When the fever overtakes him, it makes him into that disappearing essence; the fever "gave him the image of a baseball player winding up, getting ready to pitch. And he was the ball. Around and around he went, then he was flung into space for a while, dissolving in flight" (SS, p. 200). His mind comes back, goes out—and even the center cannot hold, as mere anarchy is loosed upon his world: "he could remember the two centers and distinguish between them, even though he hated them both, and he knew that the one which was only *there* was the true one, while the other was wrong, wrong, wrong" (SS, p. 222). The only unity is in the cloaca, that central sewer in which all realities drain away: "The meaningless hegemony of the involuntary" (SS, p. 214).

It is ironic that it should be only in delirium that the intellectual attains, through the perception of discreteness, the fusion he had sought in health and consciousness. Coleridge, whose genius rescued oneiric images and held them rhetorically secure, had scant patience for mystics and their assertions of privately valuable but publicly uncommunicable experience. Bowles's initial experimentation with majoun solved this aesthetic problem in *The Sheltering Sky*—the illusive good fortune of the pleasures of the drug. In subsequent works, his communication of the images that drugs produced was not always to be so happy and so clear.

The death of Port three-quarters into the book assigns full attention to his survivor, Kit. The rest of the novel relates her subsequent adventures. From the beginning Kit too had been looking for something in North Africa, though she knows her "respective aims in life were almost diametrically opposed" (SS, p. 100) to those of her husband. Hers was the pursuit of Port himself: "she still lived in a world illumined by the distant light of a possible miracle: he might yet return to her." Thus "adventure"—Gertrude Stein's "making the distant approach nearer"—is, for Kit, a search for sexual union. Her husband had been analytical and a loner; she felt "abject, and therefore, of course, furious with herself, to realize that everything depended on him, that she was merely waiting for some unlikely caprice on his part, something which might in some unforeseen manner bring him back" (SS, p. 45). But she cannot act, trapped as she is by her superstitious belief in omens, before whom "all she could hope to do was eat, sleep and cringe" (SS, p. 126)—atavistic responses bought at the suppression of intelligence. In many ways she reminds us of Sadie in Jane Bowles's story, "Camp Cataract," which was being written in Morocco while Bowles was finishing this novel: "like many others she conceived of her life as separate from herself; the road was laid out always a little ahead of her by sacred hands, and she walked down it without a question. This road, which was her life, would go on existing after her death, even as her death existed now while she still lived." [27]

But the future can also appall Kit: "in some as yet unforeseen manner time would bring about a change which could only be terrifying, since it would not be a continuation of the present" (SS, p. 207). Her phobia lasted only so long as Port lived; his death traumatizes and strangely liberates her from panic. "The element of timelessness . . . would surround her" (SS, p. 237); she who had been the spectator now lives in stasis, feeling "a vague surprise that her actions should go on so far ahead of her consciousness of them" (SS, p. 246).

Although Kit has a keen analytical ability and, in intellectual discussions, is "always the proponent of scientific method" (SS, p. 44), her basic responses are intuitive: she is active where Port is passive. As he subsides into illness, she arranges transportation from town to town, deals with the natives, and commandeers aid in a resurgence of animal vitality. Omens and the

presentiments of fate no longer immobilize her. Port
may be brought to the No of existence, but "As long as
she could ask herself the question: 'Is there anything?'
and answer: 'Yes,' she could not be dead. And there were
the sky, the sun, the sand, the slow monotonous motion
of the mehari's pace. Even if the moment came . . .
when she no longer could reply, the unanswered question would still be there before her, and she would
know that she lived. The idea comforted her" (SS, pp.
269–70). She does not need to invest the sky, the sun,
the sand with symbolic power. Even when she views the
fusion of earth and sky and cannot distinguish between
them, she views the phenomenon dispassionately. Her
omens never manifest themselves so grandly as the
naked face of nature.

From the beginning, her experience had seemed personal rather than cosmic. She was aware that Port had
not called her "Darling" in more than a year; it has
probably been longer since they had slept together. Even
in North Africa, where rooms are scarce in remote out-
posts and shabby hotels, they still find separate accom-
modations. The Moresbys have a companion in Tunner,
who is five years Port's junior, "of sturdier build, and
astonishingly handsome . . . in his late Paramount
way" (SS, p. 15), Kit admits. And he has an expressed
interest in her, if only "the acquisitive desire of the
trophy collector, nothing more" (SS, p. 254). Their
brief affair brings Kit no pleasure, merely guilt and re-
inforcement of her awareness that she wants only Port.
After Port's death, however, the immediate availability
of the solicitous Tunner may be the stimulus that drives
her headlong into the desert which he "hadn't been
able to 'take' " (SS, p. 255).

The adventures that conclude *The Sheltering Sky* almost parody sentimental novels about white ladies
wickedly trapped in a harem; it is Bowles's adroit han-

dling of such preposterousness that gives the incidents validity. (He was later to write in a notebook: "Primitivism implies ignorance of the psychological probing made possible by romanticism, whereas Neo-Classicism connotes its rejection" [HRC].) Shortly before the novel was published he wrote his publisher, "Really it is an adventure story in which the adventures take place on two planes simultaneously: in the actual desert, and in the inner desert of the spirit. The sexual adventures are like the oases, the shade is insufficient, the glare is always brighter as the journey continues. And the journey must continue—there is no oasis in which one can remain" (HRC: rough draft of letter to James Laughlin).

Whereas Norton believed in reality only after he had subverted it rhetorically, Kit responds directly to the stimuli of life. Norton supposed that the forming of a sentence could be a "therapeutic action, to avoid thinking about the thing itself"; but Kit recognizes that words bring images, the confirmation of the omens that haunt her. Deprived of Port, the navigator of her course, Kit flees, abandoning the French fort for the edge of the oasis: "instead of feeling the omens, she now would make them, *be* them herself" (SS, p. 268). When the Bedouin, Belqassim, appears, she holds up her arms to him in an embrace of the visible world. All of Port's philosophical speculations and that romantic talk about an ultimate reality beyond the sky concern her no longer. For her, life is adventure this side of the sky and beneath its shelter. Whatever quality life offers, life itself *is* and, therefore, is valuable. Hers is not the movement into silence but into music, as strange languages become melody and seduction. But hers is also the proof of Gertrude Stein's assertion that no matter how diverting is adventure, it cannot permanently sustain. And when, like the Professor in "A Distant Episode," she begins to hear words as words, she too is brought back from sensual entity to identity, into the pain of consciousness. When she begins to remember Port's words, his response to the sky as symbol ("the sky hides the night behind it, shelters the person beneath from the horror that lies above") then "the anguish began to move in her. At any moment the rip can occur, the edges fly back, and the giant maw will be revealed" (SS, p. 312). When words no longer blend musically but fracture into meaning, then she, like the Professor, knows "an access of terror."

The forced return to Oran reminds Kit that what civilization calls salvation is involvement of intellect and the regaining of self-consciousness. Terrified, she responds instinctively: she climbs aboard a streetcar and evades her would-be rescuers. When she comes to the end of the line, it is only the end of the streetcar line, that line by which civilization circumscribes life. In the desert which stretches beyond, in that nonterminating world without charts and the calibrations of civilization, there is for Kit not emptiness but the fulfillment that is addictive, "an aura of mindless contentment" (SS, p. 292), sensual, sexual, complete. "Once you have fallen victim to the spell of this vast, luminous, silent country," remarked Bowles a few years later, "no other place is quite strong enough for you, no other surroundings can provide the supremely satisfying sensation of existing in the midst of something that is absolute. You will go back, whatever the cost in discomfort and dollars, for the absolute has no price." [28]

On 22 February 1950, Alice Toklas wrote Bowles about his novel:

Dear Freddie–
    It has taken a long time to tell you how greatly I enjoyed appreciated and admired your book. I have

just reread it—there is even more in it than I suspected to justify my earlier enthusiasm. It is a considerable achievement. No novel since The Great Gatsby has impressed me as having the force, precision, delicacy that the best of Fitzgerald has until yours. Limiting yourself as you have in the number of your characters has not prevented you from completely portraying an epoch. I find one blemish—an insignificant mistake. Kit in the Sahara—my wish to compress it puts me in what Gertrude called the banal majority. If you come back to Paris in my time you will explain its inclusion. So hats off to you. Je vous felicite, monsieur. (HRC)

The comparison to Fitzgerald's finest work (a comparison made, incidentally, before interest in the Jazz Age novelist revived generally) was a brilliant stroke. Both *The Great Gatsby* and *The Sheltering Sky* have startling plots and uncommon protagonists, and each incapsulates an epoch. As Bowles himself was to say two years later: "I am writing about disease. Why? Because I am writing about today . . . not about what happens today, but about today itself" (Breit interview).

Each book studies the fulfillment of yearning. Fitzgerald explained Gatsby's pursuit by erecting the superstructure of Christian myth. But traditional myth did not well serve Bowles—we recall how unconvincing was Norton's attempt to see the encounter at Cold Point as legend. Bowles created his own evocation of the absolute in the deserts of eternity and showed, in Port, another mind that romped with God. In the cold and brilliant morning of his career Bowles illuminated Nothing and gave it the form and structure of Romance.

3

The Hours After Noon
"The Delicate Prey," *Let It Come Down,* and *The Spider's House*

Bowles completed *The Sheltering Sky* in May 1948 and sent it to Doubleday. The manuscript was not accepted: Doubleday said it was not a novel. Fortunately John Lehmann and James Laughlin each thought otherwise; and in September 1949 Lehmann published the book in England; in December, Laughlin's New Directions brought it out in America. In both countries it went through several printings; in England it was recommended by the Book Society and was chosen for the Evening Standard Book of the Month. Even before the book came out, however, word circulated about its quality, with the result that both for England and for America Bowles was encouraged to prepare collections of his short stories. It had been his first short stories, after all, that had prompted Doubleday to issue its contract for a novel. In 1950 Lehmann published *A Little Stone,* twelve of Bowles's previously published stories. That same year Random House issued *The Delicate Prey and Other Stories,*[1] which added five more stories to those from the Lehmann collection.[2]

Two stories that Bowles wrote in the year after finishing *The Sheltering Sky* are particularly interesting. The first, "The Delicate Prey," titled the American collection; the other, "The Hours after Noon," was to be one of the longest of all his stories but had to wait several years for publication. Eventually it too gave title to a short story collection, and it also helped shape Bowles's second novel, *Let It Come Down.*

After he had submitted *The Sheltering Sky,* Bowles returned to America to write the music for Tennessee Williams's *Summer and Smoke;* in December 1948 he returned to Morocco, accompanied by Williams, and it was during that voyage that he wrote "The Delicate Prey." Bowles showed the story to the playwright, who professed admiration for it but advised: " 'You mustn't publish it. Don't publish that.' And I said, 'Why not?' And he said, 'Because everyone will think you're a monster, and it will do you irreparable harm if you publish it.' Of course I didn't listen to him. . . . I wrote it for a little magazine called *Zero,* being published in Paris at the time, and I thought, 'Well, no one would ever see it except a few hundred people who read that magazine' " (Tape, LDS). That was quite a miscalculation.

In the 1947–48 winter, while working on *The Sheltering Sky,* Bowles had made his way to Timimoun in Algeria: "The food was sketchy, but I had my first camel steak there. It was an even better night when they served gazelle [the delicate prey]" (WS, p. 283). It was in Timimoun that a French captain recounted to him what would become the basic plot of the story: "how the leather sellers start out over the desert and are killed en route, and how he [the murderer] did it, by getting each one separately, pretending to go shooting, and killing them one by one, and then going on and having the leather recognized when he arrives at the other side of the desert by other Filala, and the Filala go to the French and the French turn the man over to the Filala and say, 'Do what you like with him.' So they don't have any hand in it at all. Yes, that was told me. . . . But of course I hoked it up considerably" (Tape,

LDS). Now, eleven months later, again on a ship that was carrying him back to Morocco, he was again evoking an apprehension of terror. It was not the contemplative terror of "Pages from Cold Point" but the manifested horror of "A Distant Episode," symbolized once more by "the plundering Reguibat tribes."

Partly because of the precision of detail, the story's sensational moments are as horrific as any in Bowles; the emphasis on mutilation disturbed even his fans. John Lehmann, for example, read the story in *Zero* and wrote Bowles on 17 October 1949: "I think it is extremely well done; but I must also add that my admiration (and it is great) goes out to you as an imaginative writer, and not as a purveyor of Grand Guignol" (HRC). Alice Toklas, writing on 7 December 1950 about *The Delicate Prey and Other Stories,* admonished her "Freddie": "your delicacy is perfect—precise and poignant—but the macabre fate—though inevitable that overtakes most of your prey is not to my taste" (HRC). Miss Toklas had not found the stories an advance beyond *The Sheltering Sky,* and this bothered her. When Bowles replied that they had, in general, preceded the novel (the date of "The Delicate Prey" itself was evidently not clarified), she was mollified. "It should have been said on the jacket that it was your first book instead of their foolish Gothic violence which isn't violent to us today" (HRC), she wrote him on 9 January 1951. (The Random House dust jacket insisted that the stories "share an almost Gothic preoccupation with violence—particularly that violence arising out of the clash of the Westerner with the alien world of the East.")

Gothic preoccupations are seldom historically accurate. The factual basis of the material in "The Delicate Prey" needs, therefore, to be stressed. The story is partly founded on intertribal fears and hostilities, a knowledge of which is assumed by the author. The three

leather merchants travel a real route from Tabelbala in
western Algeria, south to Taoudeni in what is now Mali,
and then southeast to Tessalit; no more is this the
geographical fantasy of *The Sheltering Sky*. Similarly
real are the group the travelers belong to (the Filala)
and the tribe they fear (the Reguibat). The murderer
who joins their party is also assignable geographically:
he is a Moungari. ("Moungar is a holy place in that part
of the world," the story tells us, "and its few residents
are treated with respect by the pilgrims who go to visit
the ruined shrine nearby.") The Filala are contrasted
with "uncouth mountain men . . . [who sweep] down
from the *hammada* upon a caravan." But even though
"the two older merchants were serious, bearded men who
liked to engage in complicated theological discussions,"
they are, as the history book—but not Bowles—remarks,
of "that terrible Sherifian family of the Filali to whom
historians give the palm for fanaticism, ferocity and
cruelty over every other dynasty that has held sway in
Morocco." [3] Thus, there may be more than hashish to
motivate the Moungari's curse at Driss, "Filali dog!"
and his belief that "It would be pleasant to inflict an
ultimate indignity upon the young Filali."

Within the story itself, however, Bowles works together many of his standard themes for his dramatic
causation. Clearly the intuition of Driss, the youngest
of the three leather merchants, would have delivered
him, had he but trusted in it. He has undoubted trust
in his sexual power and "was reasonably certain of being
able to have any lovely resident of any *quartier* [*réservé*]
whatever her present emotional entanglements"; from
his initial meeting with the Moungari he has been sus-
picious of the stranger's "small, active eyes which seemed
to take in everything and give out nothing." Furthermore, he is protectively forewarned by his dreams:
"While he had slept, a hostile presence had entered into

his consciousness. Translating into thought what he already sensed, he cried out. Since first he had seen those small, active eyes he had felt mistrust of their owner." When he temporarily flees upon intuitions "unleashed in his slumber," he is safe. But continued thought demeans them as "an absurd terror." So Bowles redramatizes the fate of those who willfully disregard their unconscious.

"The Delicate Prey" marks an advance over earlier work in its structural use of music, although "A Distant Episode" and *The Sheltering Sky*'s concluding episodes had touched on music's deception and appeal. While the three Filala travel alone, Driss nightly plays his flute, "playing whatever sad songs he could call to mind; the bright ones in his opinion belonged to the *quartier*, where one was never alone." When the Moungari first comes near them, his voice is "like a muezzin's." "In the mighty silence of the rising sun" begins the ride into death for the two Filala, though the second uncle, with classical peripeteia, goes off "singing a song from Tafilalet: it was about date-palms and hidden smiles. For several minutes Driss heard snatches of the song, as the melody reached the high notes. Then the sound was lost in the enveloping silence." When Driss returns after his temporary flight, he hears the Moungari singing. But that is not song of time and place; it is sound of a hashish reverie. "Carried along on its hot fumes, a man can escape very far from the world of meaning." Some months later, when the Moungari's crime is discovered and he is taken into the desert by the Filala from Tessalit, "he might have been singing a song for all the attention they paid to his words." Methodically they bury him alive, "until only his head remained above the earth's surface." The hashish which had encouraged the symbolic mutilation of Driss had taken the Moungari away only temporarily. Now again there would be "first warmth, then heat, thirst, fire, visions," such as the hashish had produced. But those visions that the sun will bring will also bring death. "The wind blew dust along the ground into his mouth as he sang."

The story parallels tortures. But since the Filala in Tessalit know nothing of the manner in which their friends from Tabelbala died, the Moungari's fate is not intended as redress to the mutilation of Driss. The Moungari dies horribly because he murdered their tribal brothers and stole their property. "The story had an old pattern; there was no doubt at all about the Moungari's guilt." One thread in that pattern is tribal identity, the bond that ensures the safety of caravans as they move from oasis to oasis. Another thread is the belief in the ultimate sacredness of property. From this second strand, Bowles would weave the plot for "The Hours after Noon."

In her letter to Bowles about *The Delicate Prey and Other Stories*, Alice Toklas had complimented his labeling them "detective stories": "you are so right. . . . The modern detective story . . . is the lineal descendant of the Elizabethan novels—The so-called detective and mystery stories of the last thirty years are hopelessly less eerie" (HRC: ALS, 9 Jan. 1951). She wrote Bowles again on 28 March 1951: "your explanation of your stories . . . cleared some small confusion one reader had created for herself by the seduction of following the way you so admirably solved your technical difficulties instead of discovering that your construction was based on each of your characters response to his bottom nature as Gertrude used to call it. So that the story is often a mystery until near the end to the hero himself, which makes it a really modern mystery story" (HRC).[4]

"The Hours after Noon"—a long story which Bowles had written two years earlier but which Miss Toklas had not yet read [5]—confirms her deduction. The stylistic

plainness of this novella forces the reader to focus upon
the psychological mystery where the explanation of
events is in the remembrance of rhetoric—in particular
the remembrance of two sentences, sentences which are
indeed the leveling upon life of judgment and punishment. The scene is the Pension Callender in Tangier.
The Callenders' daughter, Charlotte, is returning from
England on vacation; at the same time Monsieur Royer,
a Frenchman who formerly had stayed at the Pension
and displayed a tendency for "annoying young girls and
getting into messes," is due for a visit. Mrs. Callender's
problem is to protect her daughter without losing the
income from Royer's visit; her solution of the problem
ends in the Frenchman's murder.

Bowles dated his corrected typescript, "Fez, May 14,
1949" (HRC). But presumably the first drafts were
written elsewhere. "I was staying in Tangier, in the
Pension Callender, in that very place, and eating meals
and seeing this woman, and eating every day in that
dining room that I describe there, that's cold and windy
and the chairs make an awful scraping noise on the tile
floor. It's really journalism—in other words, it's not
filtered through memory. The place I wrote about when
I was actually in it, which I very seldom do. . . . It's
about Tangier. I do say International Zone, and the
people coming in from Gibraltar, so it's definitely
Tangier, and I was thinking of it always as Tangier"
(Tape, LDS). (Bowles believes that work in the *mise
en scène* inevitably robs a story of poetry.)

But the psychological process behind the story was not
generated by life at the Pension Callender. It had been
enunciated in *The Sheltering Sky*. While Port was
motoring to Boussif with the Lyles, his mind wandered
back to the dream that had bothered him in Oran. The
published reflection concludes: "For in order to avoid
having to deal with relative values, he had long since

come to deny all purpose to the phenomenon of existence—it was more expedient and comforting" (SS, p.
75). The manuscript, however, originally continued:

> At the same time this made it easier for him to in-
> dulge his passion for interior order. It was an all-
> important thing for him to be able at any moment to
> locate a memory. A large part of his mental energy
> went to the keeping and cross-cataloguing of a file of
> memories. This is not to say that he had access to
> the file at all times, that he could consult it at will.
> . . . But when the significant instant came, the file
> opened of itself and located the anterior items in his
> experience which were necessary to his acceptance of
> the present. . . . If any passing moment of life struck
> him as being particularly significant even as he was
> on his way through that moment, he could not rest
> until he had found the previous situation or combi-
> nation of sensations and circumstances which had
> called forth recognition and made identification an
> imperative need. (For him the *déjà-vu* was a thing
> apart, which, being a purely physical manifestation,
> had no importance.) (HRC)

"The Hours after Noon" carries an epigraph from
Baudelaire that similarly emphasizes the logic and
harmony of the awakened memory: "No matter how
incoherent the existence, the human unity is not affected." "Incoherent" is the judgment made of another's behavior and its seeming absence of pattern.
There is inevitable difficulty in assessing one's bottom
nature and solving his mystery. But, as Bowles has remarked, the Baudelaire quote "is an affirmation of the
subjective, the power of the subjective side of the personality. Because it's the same consciousness taking all
these things in, no matter how disparate they all are, the
memory will be harmonious because they all happened

to you and you saw them all" (Tape, LDS). In this novella, only Mrs. Callender and M. Royer are viewed on that level of complexity; one opens, one concludes the incidents. The other personae merely help raise into consciousness suppressed memories of the rhetoric that accounts for behavior.

At Cold Point, Norton had realized that, in his confrontation with Racky, the opening sentence would define his stand; it was a similar troubling awareness of the power of language that urged Kit Moresby's frenzied escape from words into sounds. Mrs. Callender is such a chatterbox that her daughter contemns her as superficial and scatterbrained, her irresponsibility amounting "to a denial of all values. There was no beginning and no end; anything was equal to anything else." But Charlotte has not correctly assembled the clues, and she misapprehends the value her mother places on intuition. Mrs. Callender's coy "Oh, you're a *man!* What does a man know about such things?" opens the story. She knows that her mind cannot always escape the images that surface from her unconscious; and unlike Norton, she cannot make herself happy merely by asserting that she is. "A certain nonawareness [6] of what went on around her was essential if she were to find even normal contentment." When images from her girlhood intrude, she has " 'sad days,' when she felt that life would never be right again." Like Kit Moresby's omens, those images suddenly make the world "sinister." But Mrs. Callender is also like Kit in trying, occasionally, to *be* her omens. The sinister events of the novel result from the associating of images and ideas. The associative act takes on such implications that awareness of the essential linkages of images and ideas is suppressed. But in time the images reassert themselves, and there is inescapable confrontation with one's bottom nature and his basic instinct for survival.

When Mrs. Callender hears the distant *rhaïta*, her "images had been awakened: the donkeys . . . the procession of lanterns, the native women in white"; her need to get rid of Royer connects with remembrance of his sexual needs. Later, when events turn perilously, she intuits that all depends upon "a spoken sentence, a dreadful image, but she could recall neither the sentence nor the image it had evoked." A mention of barbed wire brings back the earlier remark: "If he chases the girls around out there they'll find him in a couple of days behind a rock with a coil of wire around his neck." And we similarly remember that when Mrs. Callender could have refused Royer's coming to the pension, she had not because there was always something "which she coveted at the time: a silk scarf. . . ." Even when she gets him away, and her plan seems successful, she cannot forget the money; so, in his absence she continues to charge him for his room but equitably puts him on demi-pension.

Unlike Mrs. Callender, whose associative patterns are clearly established, Royer is infinitely complex; the solution to his mystery depends especially upon recognizing "a passage of something he once had read and loved." He himself never completely recollects it, and its source is not revealed in the story itself. The solution is to be found in Gide's *Amyntas* (of which its author wrote on 14 November 1910: "To whom could the secret value of the book speak? Only to a few rare souls; the others were disappointed.") Mrs. Callender's experience had titled Bowles's story: "It was the hours after noon that she had to beware of, when the day had begun to go towards the night, and she no longer trusted herself to be absolutely certain of what she would do next, or of what unlikely idea would come into her head." But the concern with time and change is Royer's. Throughout the story he works to reassemble Gide's line: "*Le temps*

*qui coule ici n'a plus d'heures; mais, tant l'inoccupation
de chacun est parfaite, ici devient impossible l'ennui."*
Eventually he recollects all but the last five words.
"There is more, obviously, but I don't know the rest,"
says Bowles. And he translated from memory: "The
time that flows here has no hours. But everyone's lack
of occupation is so perfect, that it doesn't seem empty.
That one is not conscious at all of there being nothing"
(Tape, LDS).

The "more" that Bowles forgot in the "Mopsus" section of *Amyntas* confirms the experience. What is
sought in North Africa? *"Oh! je sais maintenant, hors
du temps, le jardin où le temps se repose. Pays clos,
tranquille, Arcadie! . . . J'ai trouvé le lieu du repos. Ici
le geste insoucieux cueille chaque instant sans poursuite;
l'instant, inépuisablement se répète; l'heure redit l'heure
et le jour la journée."* The prelapsarian paradise is recovered sensuously and secretly—even though the Fall
had come from Knowledge. As Norton found security in
Nothingness and regained the past through the legendary
experience with Racky, so Royer would see the world as
one of mermaids and blot out time by seducing a child.

Spain had not satisfied, with its coy promises and "the
prudishness he so hated." "Here in Morocco, if love
lacked finesse, at least it was frank." But that was the
conclusion of the old roué, before the Gide sentence
had surfaced effectively. Even in her moments of greatest contempt for him, Mrs. Callender thinks Royer
is attracted to girls such as her daughter. But Royer
surrenders to his own images and dandles a young Berber girl on his knee ("she was really no more than a
child"). As he lets her examine his watch, he finds
Gide's sentence finally beginning to fill out in his mind.
Once again the cross-generational experience, the playing
with time and ignoring its implications, brings death.
For Gide, the North African fusion had been homo-

sexual and, ironically, safe. Bowles has remarked that had Royer's predilections been Gide's, there would have been less serious consequences.

To solve the mystery of the events themselves, we need to know traditional Moroccan attitudes not expressed in the novella. The Callenders' concern for money is stressed: their pension is "surprisingly empty these days" and Mr. Callender has, for eleven years, "suffered strangers to share his little paradise with him only in order to be able to keep it" (a sentence deleted in the manuscript). The financial interests of the Moroccans are not discussed; yet those concerns are equally real, as the story's plot makes clear. Royer is murdered by country people who know nothing of his past or of his history as a seducer. It is enough that the countrymen see Royer—the Christian intruder—compromising their own; and they strike. "They couldn't sell her [the girl] if she had been damaged," says Bowles. "We assume he hadn't damaged her because she wouldn't have been sitting on his knee. Probably he had just met her, but if he had been left alone with her, things would have gone further, of course. She wouldn't have stopped him, especially if he promised to give her something" (Tape, LDS).

Early in the story, before he had gotten so far in his recollection of Gide's sentence, Royer had rationalized his behavior: "There are a great many girls who have no will, like the natives here. . . . It is all the same to them, as long as they receive a gift. . . . And if they have no will, one can scarcely go against it, can one?" But those willing native girls are not the child upon his lap. The final seduction, progressing as the Gide sentence is finally being recalled, moves into perversion, as indeed the assumption that time is stoppable or recoverable is itself unnatural and delusive. All that man can logically yearn to gain is his own identity, a self-awareness of his bottom nature. To those in the company of men, one's repetitions reveal that basic insistence —and so Mrs. Callender thinks she sees into, or through, Royer. Repetitions explain us to others, never to ourselves. The loner—the usual protagonist in Bowles's fiction—must turn to surrealism, the aesthetic manifestation of his unconscious, as the best aid to detection.

Both Mrs. Callender and M. Royer are like Norton: "Receiving consciousness." But perhaps only to Royer could that reception have also brought self-awareness. Gertrude Stein herself disliked surrealism: "The surrealists still see things as every one sees them, they complicate them in a different way but the vision is that of every one else, in short the complication is the complication of the twentieth century but the vision is that of the nineteenth century." [7] Certainly Mrs. Callender's conscious ideas and unconscious notions connect in an old-fashioned vision. Bowles himself would never insist that surrealism—even in his poetry, his most surreal productions—is more than a source of material: "it's much less likely that a good work will come out of a free association than out of planning. . . . I don't think one could follow the Surrealist method absolutely, with no conscious control in the choice of material, and be likely to arrive at organic form" (Evans interview).

For Bowles's protagonists, life is a process of effecting the inner/outer reconciliation that produces harmony. Had Royer recovered Gide's sentence that lay buried within him, he might have prevented his fate. To bring before a man his resurrected unconscious is, ultimately, the highest degree of consciousness and is essential to the production of what Alice Toklas so admired: "a really modern mystery story."

In December 1949, the month that *The Sheltering Sky* was published in New York, Bowles sailed from Antwerp to Ceylon: "I had the illusion of being about to add another country, another culture, to my total experience. . . . I had a placid belief that it was good for me to live in the midst of people whose motives I did not understand; this unreasoned conviction was clearly an attempt to legitimize my curiosity" (WS, p. 297). Again upon the water and bound for an anticipated destination, he found his creative impulses suddenly detoured: "We were sailing past Tangier, past the tip there (we were only about five miles from it—less—and I could see the lights) . . . and I suddenly felt a terrible longing to be in Tangier, but I had to sail past it. So I started right in writing, *bang!* I decided to write about the very part of the land that I was going by at that second—the nearest part—and it was the beach, the grotto, the cave. . . . It was one of my favorite places there, this cave. So I started *Let It Come Down* by writing that scene when they're standing at the top of the steps and they [Dyer and Hadija] go down and see a little boy with goats. . . . That night I guess I wrote the whole thing, the whole chapter [8]. Then I began at the beginning, and I used much of the trip for planning the book. For that book I did plan. It's the only one I ever did" (Tape, LDS).

He used the three weeks at sea to work out his plot; he commenced with the characters and their motivations: "who wants what out of whom." In his notebook he drew charts and plotted alliances: "All sorts of arrows, interconnecting and so on. Why this one is that. And why the next one is that. How each one can manipulate the other, and then the others, in order to bring it to the situation that I want: the high point. And then [I thought] 'I'll leave the final section to write itself.' I did it just that way. The idea was to plan it all up to the beginning of an inevitable dénouement and write *that* section automatically. And that's the way it worked" (Tape, LDS).[8] The novel's evolution proves the Kafka epigraph for Book Three of *The Sheltering Sky*: "From a certain point onward there is no longer any turning back. That is the point that must be reached."

To reach that point was not easy. Bowles spent nearly two years on this novel, more time than that given any of his other works, and again he constructed fictive reality by a journalistic attention to the details of life met with as he wrote the book itself. "It was completely surface-built, down to the details of the decor, choice of symbolic materials on the walls, and so on. The whole thing was planned. It had to be. It was an adventure story, after all, in which the details had to be realistic. There would have been no other way of lending it any semblance of reality. It's a completely unreal story, and the entire book is constructed in order to lead to this impossible situation at the end" (Evans interview). Had writing become only contrivance and not an act of discovery? [9] Gertrude Stein would have disapproved: "adventure has really nothing to do with creation, because the distant thing being brought nearer ceases to have any existence inside in one and therefore adventure has no relation to creation" (*What Are Masterpieces*, pp. 63–64).

Eventually, Bowles's working-out of the novel brought him to the same conclusion; and even when he was writing an adventure, he felt successful only when he treated it as romance. He wrote his mother from Xauen on 26 July 1951,

with a novel the work is a good deal more than just consecrating so many hours of the day to sitting at a desk writing words;—it is living in the midst of the artificial world one is creating, and letting no detail of everyday life enter sufficiently into one's mind to become more real than or take precedence over what one is inventing. That is, living in the atmosphere of the novel has to become and stay more real than living in one's own life. Which is why it is almost impossible to work in a city, or with people around. At least, for me. Under the latter conditions I write mere words, staying outside what I am doing, and anyone knows that is not the way to write a novel,— at least, not a novel that people are going to become engrossed in. (HRC)

Avoiding "contact with the outside," he escaped from Tangier in order to keep clear within himself a contrived world revolving upon connivance. For in his fictive city, residents smuggle, spy, embezzle, cheat, deceive, and seduce—and confirm Lempriere's eighteenth-century appraisal of the Moorish character (and, by extension, that of the expatriate there):

> we must take into our consideration the natural effects of a total want of education, a most rigidly arbitrary government, and a climate calculated, as far as climate has influence, to stimulate and excite the vicious passions, as well as by its debilitating and relaxing influence to weaken and depress the nobler energies of the mind. . . . In such a state of things the traveller is not to be surprized if he observes most of the vices of savage nations grafted upon those of luxury and indolence; if he observes superstition, avarice, and lust, the leading features of character, with their natural concomitants, deceit and jealousy; he is not to be surprized if he finds but little of the amiable attachments and propensities, little of friendship or social union with each other, since the nature of the government, and the habits of his private life, are calculated to inspire each man with a distrust and suspicion of his neighbour. (A *Tour from Gibraltar*, pp. 282–83)

The novel's International Zone city of Tangier, how-ever, escapes the "rigidly arbitrary government" that Lempriere had encountered in Marrakech. "It was one of the charms of the International Zone," says Bowles's narrative voice, "that you could get anything you wanted if you paid for it. Do anything, too, for that matter;— there were no incorruptibles. It was only a question of price" (LICD, p. 13).[10] The expatriate Daisy de Valverde says "It's a madhouse, of course. A complete, utter madhouse. I only hope to God it remains one" (LICD, p. 16). But even she is not prepared for the madness which ends Dyar's sanity and the novel.

We regard the characters and incidents of this novel properly only if we remember an attitude that Bowles has consistently maintained toward Tangier: "I think it appeals particularly to those with a strong residue of infantilism in their character. There is an element of make-believe in the native life as seen from without (which is the only viewpoint from which we can ever see it, no matter how many years we may remain). It is a toy cosmos whose costumed inhabitants are playing an eternal game of buying and selling. . . . when you hud-dle or recline inside the miniature rooms of the homes you are immediately back in early childhood, playing house, an illusion which is not dispelled by the tiny tables and tea glasses, the gaudy cushions and the lack of other furniture. The beggars come by and sing outside the door, each one with his own little song, and the forgotten but suddenly familiar sensation of being far *inside* is complete." [11] Gertrude Stein would have un-derstood: "Romance is the outside thing, that remains the outside thing and remaining there has its own exist-ing and so although it is outside it is inside because it being outside and staying outside it is always a thing to be felt inside" (*What Are Masterpieces*, p. 64).

In the novel itself, Eunice Goode, a lesbian writer,

distinguishes between "her own familiar little cosmos" and "the rest of the world" (LICD, p. 48). Hers is "always the aching regret for a vanished innocence, a nostalgia for the early years of life" (LICD, p. 49). But the penalty of such a vision is emphasized by her grotesque appearance and behavior. She is "a comic character. . . . Dressed in a manner which accentuated the deficiencies of her body, wherever she went she was a thing rather than a person" (LICD, p. 97). She is a caricature like Mrs. Lyle and useful to the novel's machinations, paralleling and competing with the concerns of the hero.

Bowles's major difficulty with the book was conceptual: how can writing be a continuing act of self-discovery for the author himself if he must plot in advance the discoveries that must be made? Once Bowles began to "live in story," he focused upon Dyar; and that caravansary of other characters moves out of sight. No more could Bowles weave the tapestry portrait of Tangerine life.

This structural dilemma is mirrored in the contradictory attitudes taken toward free will and the *acte gratuit*. The Baudelaire epigraph for "The Hours after Noon" had begun: "If one could awaken all the echoes of one's memory simultaneously, they would make a music, delightful or sad as the case might be, but logical and without dissonances." There is within Dyar himself such a harmony; and Bowles uses his hero's sensitivity to music to bridge unconscious responses and visible acts.

Though Dyar can react to Tangerine life as "episodes of varying sorts of noise" (LICD, p. 69), he becomes changed by the sounds of nature there: "the dry slapping of an enormous fanshaped branch (it covered and uncovered a certain group of stars as it waved back and forth) was like the distant slamming of an old screen door." These natural sounds "washed through him"

and, in their ghostly harmony, gave him "the infinites-
imal promise of a possible change" (LICD, pp. 128–29).
Later he recalls this harmonic moment as that which
moved him to a conviction that "something's going to
happen" (LICD, p. 171); but he knows that he himself
must strike the galvanic chord. That chord is sounded by
majoun, associating objects, atmosphere, and ideas in a
paradox of sound: "all these things were playing a huge,
inaudibile music that was rising each second toward a
climax which he knew would be unbearable" (LICD,
p. 222). Later, still *m'hashish*,[12] "he found himself entering a region of his memory which . . . he thought had
been lost forever. It began with a song . . . the only song
that had ever made him feel really happy." It repos-
sessed childhood and its shelter when "like the sky, his
mother was spread above him. . . . Her voice was above,
and she was all around; that way there was no possible
danger in the world" (LICD, p. 239).

The moment Dyar recognizes that he himself must
strike the proper chord, that moment brings together the
novel's structural images and concepts: "his great problem right now was to escape from his cage, to discover
the way out of the fly-trap, to strike the chord inside
himself which would liberate those qualities capable of
transforming him from a victim into a winner" (LICD,
p. 172). In *The Sheltering Sky* Port had built a cage to
save himself from love, an immurement bought at the
expense of Kit. But Dyar, a New York bank clerk, has
come to Tangier "to exchange one cage for another"
(LICD, p. 9). Daisy de Valverde examines his hand the
night of his arrival and sees in it "No sign of anything,
to be quite honest, I've never seen such an empty hand.
It's terrifying" (LICD, p. 22). But Dyar does not begin
the novel by seeing himself as having the worst of hands
and lives: "There never was any mass production to
compare with the one that turns out human beings—all

the same model, year after year, century after century, all alike, always the same person. . . . You might say there's only one person in the world, and we're all it" (LICD, p. 23), he asserts cynically. Being cut to the universal pattern is privately disquieting: "even to himself he felt supremely anonymous" (LICD, p. 114).

His interior emptiness had always required formal definition. When Dyar finally goes to work at the travel agency and is told, "Well, here's your cage" (LICD, p. 72) he is reassured by the evidence of a business world he thought he had wanted to escape. "I want to feel I'm alive, I guess" (LICD, p. 24) is his only announced goal. In time he will define life as "all the qualities of the earth from which it springs, plus the consciousness of having them" (LICD, p. 269). Dyar's schemes give him hope, "like a prisoner who had broken through the first bar of his cell, but was still inside" (LICD, p. 143). When Tangier itself becomes to him a "cage of cause and effect, the cage to which others held the keys" (LICD, p. 265), he has himself smuggled into the Spanish Zone. "It was possible he was still in the cage—that he could not know—but at least no one else had the keys" (LICD, p. 266).

The title emphasizes the difficulty in comprehending plausible cause-and-effect relationships and suggests how Bowles himself would have us regard the novel's events: "I got that [title] sitting on a train, going up from Galle to Colombo. I had a copy of Shakespeare's plays with me, and I was reading *Macbeth*. And suddenly I came to the scene where they stabbed Banquo, and I remembered how much I had always loved that from childhood. . . . Conversation is being made about something else completely different, and the attack is out of the blue. The conversation has nothing to do with what's going to happen or does happen. The first murderer who kills Banquo has his counterpart not in any particular character but in the behavior more or less of everyone in the novel. Everyone's so busy betraying everyone else and looking after himself. (*Betrayal* isn't exactly the right word.) There's a great deal of the kind of action that the prestidigitator does: keeping the hands busy so you won't really see the important thing, and then the attack comes. One is stabbed in the back for having watched the hands."

He sought for the accurate term: "*Treachery*—that's the word! It seems to me that the quotation shows the exact kind of treachery that we find in Tangier (in the book) on the part of the people. It's an atmosphere of treachery. Everyone's working behind everyone else's back and you never know when the blow is coming, and then it turns out that it isn't the hero [Dyar] who gets the blow dealt him—*he deals it*, without meaning to. So he betrays himself. The worst act of treachery is not committed against him at all—he commits it" (Tape, LDS).

But why does he commit it? Dyar's world divides into winners and victims. An entry in Bowles's notebook explains: "Dyar must get growing feeling of being sought after, preyed upon—a victim" (HRC). Being a winner "was a matter of conviction, of feeling like one, of knowing you belonged to the caste, of recognizing and being sure of your genius" (LICD, p. 147). Understandably, Dyar refuses to accept "the same old sensation of not being involved, of being left out, of being beside reality rather than in it" (LICD, p. 240). As murderer and as "winner" he reaches the delusive conclusion: "A place in the world, a definite status, a precise relationship with the rest of men. Even if it had to be one of open hostility, it was his, created by him" (LICD, p. 311).

Daisy had warned Dyar, "You have an empty hand, and vacuums have a tendency to fill up. Be careful what goes into your life" (LICD, p. 232). What has gone in is, of course, the hashish to which she has introduced him. "One thinks one's making sense, and so one is, I daresay, but in a completely different world of thought," Daisy tells him. "You find absolutely new places inside yourself, places you feel simply couldn't be a part of you, and yet there they are" (LICD, pp. 219–21). Kif reveals "a corner of his existence he had known was there, but until now had not been able to reach; at present, having discovered it, he also knew he would be able to find his way back another time. Something was being completed; there would be less room for fear" (LICD, p. 226). A notebook entry reads: "With relation to hashish, Dyar wants to have a logical reason for feeling in the midst of unreality. Thus when he fails to achieve contact with situations he can ascribe it to having smoked" (HRC).

But hashish also liberates from Dyar's unconscious a monstrous force, somehow bound to memories of his childhood. "A mass of words had begun to ferment inside him, and now they bubbled forth. 'Many Mabel damn. Molly Daddy lamb. Lolly dibble up-man. Dolly little Dan,' he whispered, and then he giggled." This gibberish is his accompaniment as he drives a nail into the head of his sleeping friend, Thami. When we ask Why did he do it? we are reminded that Dyar has escaped the cage of cause and effect. If there is a cause assignable, it is hashish. "The nail was as firmly embedded as if it had been driven into a cocoanut. 'Merry Mabel dune.' The children were going to make a noise when they came out at recess-time. The fire rattled, the same insistent music that could not be stilled, the same sky-rockets that would not hurry to explode. . . . Someone had shut the bureau drawer he was lying in and gone away, forgotten him. The great languor. The great slowness. The night had sections filled with repose, and there were places in time to be visited, faces to forget, words to understand, silences to be studied" (LICD, pp. 301–2). So we return to the moment when Port pierced the fine fabric of the sheltering sky and took repose; but this time it is, as the title to this section of *Let It Come Down* points out, "Another Kind of Silence."

Just as the mention of barbed wire rang through Mrs. Callender's memory and revived the sentence that explained Royer's disappearance, so this horrible deed too redounds from an earlier and innocent thought. When Dyar had sat in the Beidouai garden, listening to the music of nature—perhaps the turning moment in his Moroccan experience—the sound he heard was compared to the slamming of a door. Near the end of his sojourn he is bothered that the door of the shack in which he and Thami have taken refuge bangs in the wind. "A little piece of wood, a hammer and one nail could arrange everything: the barrier between himself and the world outside would be much more real" (LICD, pp. 262–63), he thinks. And when he, *m'hashish*, drives the nail instead into Thami's head, that act does indeed effectively close the door on his cage.

But what are we to make of the gibberish chanted while the deed is done, those images resurrected from infancy? Surrealist dreams embody images that become symbols and, in their implications, reveal that bottom nature which, as Gertrude Stein remarked, makes us like millions who have preceded us and millions more who will follow. We do not possess sufficient evidence to determine Dyar's bottom nature; but enough is supplied to deny that the act of murder is gratuitous. We are forced to accept that his act is a melodramatic enigma—for, as Miss Stein emphasized, melodrama invariably disguises that bottom nature.

Bowles had once considered presenting his hero more understandably, for he himself had begun the novel with no doubt about Dyar's motivations. The notebook recounts:

At some crucial moment in later section, Dyar is put in contact with his early life—not reliving it, far too distant for that—like looking through telescope wrong way around—but very intimate, as if each gesture were now to be explained, completed, given its excuse, meaning. (Gesture, scene, situation) or seen in its final and true light & perspective.

But the result of all this is that everything is merely a repetition and was already complete, definite, unalterable. Meaning having been implicit in the fact of its having occurred or existed. Feeling of contentment, (fulfillment) comes, however, with explanation of new understanding which, changing nothing, changes everything. (HRC)

Bowles did indeed put this section into the book (pp. 269–70)—but as a kif experience where the given perspective is delusional.

There is no doubt that Dyar's dichotomy of character (the limbo figure with discrete acts vs. the model man with acts working to a pattern) was to have enriched the novel. *The Sheltering Sky* had considered these two approaches to life serially: first Port resurrected identity via the patterns of romance; then Kit, via the improvised responses of adventure. But Kit's hegira proved that, ultimately, there is no escape from the awakened memory; the *acte gratuit* is itself a fantasy. Dyar himself wants existence "cut down to the pinpoint of here and now, with no echoes reverberating from the past, no tinglings of expectation from time not yet arrived" (LICD, p. 269); then, within minutes, he concedes to himself that all his past is "an unalterable part of the pattern. . . . And so everything turned out to have been already complete, its form decided and irrevocable" (LICD, p. 270). Peculiarly, these conclusions precede by a few hours the murderous act itself. Even after Dyar's acceptance of pattern, *Let It Come Down* rejects conclusion and attempts to show that the *acte gratuit* can indeed be. We are forced to accept the murder of Thami as the existential act: the assertion of will in a void, and the repudiation of the Baudelaire epigraph.

However horrific the events in *Let It Come Down,* and however devious the affairs of its expatriate inhabitants, the International City of Tangier remained a safe island of the bizarre in a colorful land—safe, that is, until the early 1950s when political unrest in French Morocco made all of Morocco alien for foreigners. The French "were specifically anti-American in their behavior, because they believed the arms that the Moroccans [particularly, the Istiqlal—at that time the party of national independence] used against them came from the American bases" (WS, p. 323); the Moroccans themselves believed that the American government supported the French.

Bowles has lived most of his North African years in Tangier, yet his favorite city remains Fez. "To grasp the fascination of the place one has to be the sort of person who likes to lose himself in a crowd and be pushed along by it, not caring where to or for how long. He must be able to attain relaxation in the idea of being helpless in the face of that crowd, he must know how to find pleasure in the outlandish, and see beauty where it is most unlikely to appear." [13] Now that the country was on the verge of civil war, "Fez was on my mind. What would it be like to see one's city, the only city one knows, falling to pieces from day to day before one's eyes?" (WS, p. 324). Fez would typify the national struggle at its most complex: "the people of Fez were well known to be the most devious and clever Moslems in Morocco. But scheming in their own traditional fashion was one thing, and being caught between the diabolical French colonial secret police and the pitiless Istiqlal was another" (SH, p. 49).

Although Bowles is now widely regarded as an authority on Moroccan life, he brought the Moslem world effectively into his fiction only after he had worked there as a journalist. In *The Sheltering Sky*, it is the landscape of North Africa, rather than its inhabitants, which arouses the consciousness of the American travelers to self-awareness. *Let It Come Down* briefly recounted Moroccan life, but always in association with expatriates. We glimpse Thami in his domestic environment but are reminded that Thami is not typical: he has broken with too many customs to retain his identity as a Moslem; he is the flimsy bridge between the native culture and the alien-imposed.

At least twice, however, Bowles had attempted earlier to get into the Moroccan mind and dramatize its point-of-view: "A Thousand Days for Mokhtar," a 1949 story that relies upon an O. Henry–type ending for its effect, and "The Successor," a 1950 work, written as a diversion in Ceylon while Bowles was occupied with *Let It Come Down*. Both are unusually simplistic. Bowles has done little more in them than give some of his abiding concerns a local habitation and a Moslem name, as though local color could effectively depict the textured complexity of a civilization. It is understandable that in early 1952 he should have concluded: "I don't think we're likely to get to know the Moslems very well, and I suspect that if we should we'd find them less sympathetic than we do at present. And I believe the same applies to their getting to know us. At the moment they admire us for our technique; I don't think they could find more than that compatible. Their culture is essentially barbarous, their mentality that of a purely predatory people. It seems to me that their political aspirations, while emotionally understandable, are absurd, and any realization of them will have a disastrous effect on the rest of the world" (Breit interview).

Two years later, however, when Bowles came to write his third novel, he had gained confidence about his insight into Moroccan life. "The fact that I've done all these pieces for *Holiday* has been one of the brakes on my writing fiction, all through the fifties. I wrote some, of course. I would have written more, I think, had I not had to do all these articles" (Tape, LDS). But the journalistic assignments, forcing him to explain Morocco and its inhabitants to a curious America, crystalized some of his otherwise unstructured impressions. In particular we can look to his June 1954 review of Peter Mayne's *The Alleys of Marrakesh*, in which he praised Mayne

> because he understands the inhabitants and is aware of the fact that liking them is not enough. He knows how to make his personality malleable, so that it can fit the form of the most unlikely circumstances, and at the same time how to maintain an inflexible will. . . . On the one hand, the outsider must manage to convince the natives that he is not just another detested Nazarene come to exploit them; he must make them believe that he considers them people like himself. At the same time, since any show of good-will is so generally interpreted by Moslems as mere weakness, he must preserve his personal integrity . . . if the necessary severity is not accompanied by great finesse, the newcomer simply slips back into the category of unwanted colonial.

Bowles commended Mayne for seeing the Moroccans "as real people rather than symbols of nostalgia for a lost simplicity of soul, or exotic and amusing objects of decoration." That review enunciates many attitudes that were to be dramatized in *The Spider's House*. Particularly was Bowles pleased by Mayne's "having completely ignored the political 'situation.' " [14]

Bowles's personal life had also become enriched by warm friendship with some young Moroccans, particularly through acquaintance with M. Abdessalem Ktiri, "an unusually pleasant Fassi gentleman with a great number of sons and daughters. At M. Ktiri's I now met several young men, all natives of Fez, who in another decade would be occupying top posts in the Moroccan government. At the moment they were attending the College Moulay Idriss [in Fez]. I also met Ahmed Yacoubi, the future painter" (WS, p. 280); Yacoubi was the son of a religious healer in Fez.[15] Undoubtedly Yacoubi's friendship exerted great influence on Bowles's developing awareness of Moslem life. Bowles encouraged the young man to paint, helped arrange New York and North African exhibitions for his work, and made of Yacoubi a companion for many journeys through Europe and to Ceylon. They went to Istanbul together in September 1953, where Yacoubi turned out "to be a kind of passkey to the place. He knows how to deal with Moslems, and he has the Moslem sense of seemliness and protocol. He has also an intuitive gift for the immediate understanding of a situation and at the same time is completely lacking in reticence or inhibitions" (HAG, p. 74).[16] Bowles's new comprehension of Morocco would not invalidate his past concerns. Though he was writing in the midst of political strife that, even as he published his novel, would be unresolved, at no time would he be a political novelist. The events in Fez in 1954 were the appropriate backdrop against which the drama of human personality again takes place. But this time the cast accurately includes the Moslem as well as his American visitor.

On 20 August 1953, Sidi Mohammed, the ruler of Morocco, was summarily deposed by the French and exiled—first to Corsica, then to Madagascar. August twentieth "was the eve of the great religious festival, the Aid el Kebir, or the Feast of the Sacrifice, in commemoration of Abraham's sacrifice of his son Isaac. This festival ranks as one of the most solemn in Islam. There is no Moor so poor that he will not find some way of procuring for that day a sheep that he has to sacrifice (and, finally, to consume as a rare treat). But to assure the validity of the feast—which, if properly performed, will be a good omen for the subsequent year —the Sultan, as Imam, must personally sacrifice the first sheep." [17] The French political act, preventing that ritual sacrifice, was automatically an act of sacrilege. The same afternoon that the French in Rabat arrested the Sultan, there was attendant activity in Fez. That night the French rounded up the *oulema*—the learned doctors of Islamic law, whose right it was traditionally to name the Sultan—and ordered them to be present the following morning to sign the *beia*, the decree issued by the *oulema* to proclaim the new and legitimate Sultan. The French had decided that the new Sultan would be the elderly uncle of Sidi Mohammed, Moulay Arafa, "who can neither read nor write, nor yet do simple arithmetic, nor speak French" (Landau, p. 312). (Two years later, in November 1955—the month that *The Spider's House* was published—Sidi Mohammed was returned from exile, and the war of independence moved into a new phase.)

Bowles was in Rome, working on a film, in the fateful August that the Sultan was deposed. In Tangier in the fall of 1954, he began his novel, and he decided to set his incidents about the time of the 1954 Aid el Kebir. "What right has anybody got to make a feast when the Sultan is in prison in the middle of the ocean?" asks the potter in the novel. " 'But it's a sin not to have the Aïd el Kebir,' said Amar slowly. 'Which is greater, the Sultan or Islam?' The potter glared at him. 'Sin! Sin!' he cried. 'Is there any sin worse than living without our

Sultan? Like dogs? Like heathens, *kaffirine*? There are no sins any more, I tell you! It doesn't matter what anyone does now. Sins are finished!' " (SH, p. 114). In a note for what became page 387 of the published novel, Bowles wrote: "Bring up sins are finished motif—if no sin, everything is sin. If man can decide for himself what is sin, what is not, he has committed the ultimate sin, that of striving to become God" (HRC).

That argument gives title to Book Two of the novel and emphasizes the paradox. What the French had, in 1953, badly timed in ignorance, the Istiqlal wishes in 1954 to commemorate deliberately. If the French action prevented the proper observance of the 1953 feast (and inevitably brought about the terrors and uncertainties of the subsequent year), then the political insurgents of Morocco wish to override the admonition of Islamic law and make nonobservance an act of political support. Tension builds in the kingdom and in the novel, as the devout Moslem is torn between two equally unacceptable choices. He may abstain from the feast (thus offending Allah but escaping the wrath of the Istiqlal by showing his support for the Sultan in exile) or he may make the sacrifice (even though the Imam is now a detested impostor and public worship has become a tacit indication of support for the French).

This valid tension in the situation and the setting obviated any need for gimmicks or melodrama to achieve interest and imply complexity. Bowles no longer required his fiction to work out an identity for himself or to solve problems. *The Spider's House* is the longest, but was the most quickly written, of any of his novels. Living in the Casbah of Tangier, he "had a new routine worked out, which was a thermos of coffee by the bed. When it got light, I sat up and began working. . . . My window was right on this little alley, and people came clattering through, selling milk and screaming—it was noisy as

soon as dawn came. It was quiet as the grave all night—
no sound except the ocean breaking" (Tape, LDS).
Perhaps like Stenham, he realized that "a judgment
reached later in the day could go wide of the mark
because then he had the use of his equipment for self-
deception, whereas at this hour it had not begun to
function" (SH, p. 233). The resultant novel is "a sort
of *apologia*. Not for anything that one can ever do
again. It's simply an evocation of that which has been
lost. We'll never have it again. It's finished, it's smashed,
it's broken. We've killed God and that's the end of it.
There won't ever be that again" (Evans interview).

The published novel is the story of Stenham, an
American expatriate novelist who has lived for several
years in Fez; Polly (Lee) Veyron, an American tourist;
and Amar, a Moroccan youth, all of whom meet in the
autumn of 1954 in a Fez that is torn with the beginnings
of civil war. The manuscripts of *The Spider's House* suggest that it began as a novel entirely about Amar, the
illiterate fifteen-year-old second son of Si Driss.[18] The
family is "Chorfa, descendents of the Prophet," and
like many Chorfa Amar has the *baraka*,[19] but intensely
so: "In his family the *baraka* was very strong, so powerful that in each generation one man had always made
healing his profession" (SH, p. 19). In Amar that gift is
reinforced by "the gift of knowing what was in the
hearts of other men" (SH, p. 88). His father has insisted
that he know well "the moral precepts of Islam" (SH,
p. 19); and thus Amar believes that he will learn his
own destiny "merely by doing what it had been written
that he would do" (SH, p. 16), for "if men dared take
it upon themselves to decide what was sin and what was
not, a thing which only Allah had the wisdom to do,
then they committed the most terrible sin of all, the
ultimate one, that of attempting to replace Him" (SH,
p. 387). Such acceptance of destiny does not make him

lethargic. It was his excited embrace of life which, while he was still a child, had won from him dying grandfather the blessing which was expected to go to his elder brother. And now at fifteen he rejoices that "there was the whole vast earth waiting, the live, mysterious earth, that belonged to him in a way it could belong to no one else, and where anything at all might happen" (SH, p. 29). Had not his father told him that a happy moment in nature is a presage of paradise and encouragement for the soul to strive to be worthy of going there?

Obedient as he may be, and taught by his father that all *politique* is lies — and "All lies are sins" (SH, p. 28) — he wants to "feel the joy that comes from knowing that evil is punished in this world as well as in the next, that justice and truth must prevail on earth as well as hereafter" (SH, p. 72). But he accepts what he has been taught: "Man was meant to consider only the present; to be preoccupied with the future, either pleasantly or with anxiety, implied a lack of humility in the face of Providence, and was unforgivable" (SH, pp. 272–73). In the beginning of the novel he takes refuge in daydreams and fantasies of revenge appropriate to a young Moslem. But this *Bildungsroman* brings him to a more practical wisdom, and he learns respect for the mysterious Nazarenes who, seemingly accidentally (but evidently by the will of Allah), come into his life and alter its direction. "The world was something different from what he had thought it. . . . He would know, but nothing would have meaning, because the knowing was itself the meaning" (SH, p. 399) — that is his final discovery.

In 1953, Bowles had concluded that "The Turks are the only Moslems I have seen who seem to have got rid of that curious sentiment (apparently held by all followers of the True Faith), that there is an inevitable and hopeless difference between themselves and non-

Moslems. Subjectively, at least, they have managed to bridge the gulf created by their religion, that abyss which isolates Islam from the rest of the world" (HAG, p. 88). Among the notes for *The Spider's House* is the cryptic: "How culture could not produce such a person as Amar. What kind?" (HRC). That was the problem: how could Amar be made simultaneously typical and atypical? How could he remain a devout Moslem and yet wish to bridge his world to a Nazarene one?

Like many solitary young men, Amar is looking for "the possible friend . . . in whom he could confide, who could understand him" (SH, p. 71). "It was part of his nature to push his way to the inside and yet at the last moment to remain on the outside" (SH, p. 131). His going, solitarily, to a café "just outside the walls" is not unexpected. But the café is reached "by going across a small wooden footbridge" (SH, p. 133). He sits in the back room and stares outside at a pool of water. "It was that happy frame of mind into which his people could project themselves so easily . . . anything that occupied the eye without engaging the mind, was of use in sustaining it. It was the world behind the world, where reflection precludes the necessity for action . . ." (SH, p. 135). Then he goes down to the pool and there discovers a dragonfly trapped on the surface, its irridescent wings weighed down by moisture. He rolls up his pant legs, goes into the water, and lifts the dragonfly into the air so that it can dry its wings. "Then he stood there in the water looking at it and grinning, because its two enormous eyes seemed to be returning his stare. Perhaps it was thanking him. 'How great are the works of Allah,' he whispered" (SH, p. 139). And the dragonfly flies away.

That solitary moment has not gone unobserved. Two Americans, Stenham and Polly, have also come across that footbridge and gone into the room overlooking the pond. For Polly, who insisted "that no one must ever go back" and that "all living things were in process of evolution . . . an endless journey from the undifferentiated toward the precise, from the simple toward the complex . . . from the darkness toward the light" (SH, p. 314), Amar is merely "the model for all the worst paintings foreigners did in Italy a hundred years ago. *Boy at Fountain, Gipsy Carrying Water Jar*" (SH, p. 251). Stenham too would rather turn life into a tableau: he "would have liked to prolong the status quo because the décor that went with it suited his personal taste" (SH, p. 286). Later, after Amar has become so resolutely a part of their Fez experience, Stenham "marveled at the mysterious way in which the pieces of the world were tied together, that it should have been a purely sentimental detail like a dragonfly struggling in a pool of water, a thing exterior to any conceivable interpretation of Moslem dogma, which had made it possible for him to suspect, even unconsciously, the presence of hidden riches" (SH, p. 329). To Amar it had all been the confirmation that there was a plan, that Allah is indeed the master plotter.

Plotting occurs, of course, only in time. And awareness of time's passage, says Bowles, "can exist only if something is going on in the mind which is not completely a reflection of what is going on immediately outside" (SH, p. 53). The political events in Fez bring Amar to that awareness; and he, in turn, provokes the varying attitudes that the Americans and English in Fez take toward the past and progress. Polly sees him only as a "complete young barbarian," innocence that is self-defeating and must be corrupted to be modernized. Therefore she gives him money secretly to buy a gun and get into the struggle. Stenham places a value on that primitive intelligence. Amar "personified Stenham's infantile hope that time might still be halted and man sent back to his origins" (SH, p. 345). His is not entirely an altruistic attitude: "living among a less evolved people enabled him to see his own culture from the outside, and thus to understand it better" (SH, p. 251).

Stenham is a novelist of some reputation and discernment. His experiences so frequently parallel Bowles's own that one inclines to fuse them into an entity. When Stenham asserts that "a man must at all costs keep some part of himself outside and beyond life," we hear Bowles speaking in his own voice. "If he should ever for an instant cease doubting, accept wholly the truth of what his senses conveyed to him, he would be dislodged from the solid ground to which he clung and swept along with the current, having lost all objective sense, totally involved in existence" (SH, p. 203). These meditations upon the relationship of inside to outside—reminiscent of Gertrude Stein's own puzzlements on the problem— are characteristic of Stenham-Bowles: "No matter what went on outside, the mind forged ahead, manufacturing its own adventures for itself, and who was to know where reality was, inside or out?" (SH, p. 197). Similarly, Stenham speaks from Bowles's experience when there is analysis of the Moroccans: "in their minds one thing doesn't come from another thing. Nothing is a result of anything. Everything merely *is*, and no questions asked. . . . Everything's explained by the constant intervention of Allah. And whatever happens had to happen, and was decreed at the beginning of time, and there's no way even of imagining how anything could have been different from what it is" (SH, p. 187).

But Stenham's insight is not always so percipient as is Bowles's. Not only does he oversimplify; he is one who cuts and runs. When he had been a communist, "Nothing had importance save the exquisitely isolated cosmos of his own consciousness" (SH, p. 195). There is a residue to such solipsism, "and all existence, including his own hermetic structure from which he had observed existence, had become absurd and unreal" (SH, p. 196). He doubts therefore the quality of Amar. Time brings him to a fuller appreciation, but even then he does not understand his extraordinary effect upon the child and the moral responsibility his exerted charm has incurred. In his notebook Bowles analyzed this dilemma in note for a concluding scene: "Amar's intuitive undefined feeling that these half-drunken men [the native insurgents] are not going to make the new life, because they are without love or understanding. Haunted by memory of Nazarene. No word or sentence he had said to him, —only the way he had been, talked—the fact he had understood" (HRC). Stenham professes respect for the Koran because it embodies his personal regard for the past; he has no interest in its moral pronouncements or attitudes, for he really believes that Moroccans are much like other people and that "the differences were largely those of ritual and gesture, that even the fine curtain of magic through which they observed life was not a complex thing, and did not give their perceptions any profundity" (SH, p. 6); and so for him, bridging cultures is merely playing games.

Amar does not comprehend this amusement in a willed self-deception; had not the games and tricks of Fez been always directed against another and never at oneself? He has seen a nimbus about Stenham's blond head and secretly believes it is his inherited power of *baraka* "which had made it possible for him to recognize the sign and behave accordingly" (SH, p. 268). It is a false sign, falsely read. For Stenham does not reciprocate trust. At the novel's end, when Stenham and Polly are leaving Fez behind to civil war, Amar asks to go with them as far as Meknes, to join his mother and sister there. Stenham thinks the boy wishes merely to continue their attachment and is lying about the presence of his family. Deluding himself about his own charm, he waves back at Amar as the boy runs after the departing car. Only a few days earlier, at the festival in the mountains, Stenham, "lying back to see only the sky," realized he "had no compulsion to save the world. . . . He merely wanted to save himself. That was more than enough work for one lifetime" (SH, p. 344). For him, the experience in Fez is over, and Polly is now his interest.

But for the boy who, despite his faith, tried to build a bridge to meet the infidel, that separation comes with sadness; and he would never be so sure again of the virtues of his inherited power. Once again the colonial has corrupted the native and plundered the virtue he had gone to protect and commemorate. Once again we are reminded of *The Great Gatsby*—this time, its conclusion: "the orgastic future that year by year recedes before us. It eluded us then, but that's no matter—to-morrow we will run faster, stretch out our arms farther. . . . And one fine morning—So we beat on, boats against the current, borne back ceaselessly into the past." *The Spider's House* concludes: "Amar was running after the car. It was still there, ahead of him, going further away and faster. He could never catch it, but he ran because there was nothing else to do" (SH, p. 405). Now it is the unattainable future, rather than the unrecoverable past, that eludes us. Appropriately, Bowles quoted from the Koran as epigraph to his novel: "The likeness of those who choose other patrons than Allah is as the likeness of the spider when she taketh unto herself a house, and lo! the frailest of all houses is the spider's house, if they but knew." The spider's web is not only the most fragile of bridges; it is the most effective of traps.

4

The Twilight Hour of the Storyteller
The Translations, A *Hundred Camels in the Courtyard*, and "The Time of Friendship"

Ever since childhood, when his mother read nightly to him from Hawthorne, Poe, or Lewis Carroll, Bowles has been fascinated by the magic of storytelling. It was not unexpected, therefore, that when he first visited Morocco he should be taken with its resident storytellers, those men who at the close of day recited in the public square—particularly the Djemaa el Fna of Marrakech— wondrous and "rather grandiose stories about the Sultan and his daughter and the rich Jew who tries to get her . . . [stories] very full of plot. There's lots of magic and transformation" (Tape, LDS). The stories returned him to the world of A *Thousand and One Nights*; this was the pageantry of the Arab world and its childlike appeal to whose immediacy he was ever responsive.

The friendship with Ahmed Yacoubi, besides giving Bowles an insight that made possible *The Spider's House*, also gave him awareness of another kind of Moroccan story and storyteller. These were new stories, not traditional ones, and they were told by the young Moroccans Bowles met, and not by the professional storytellers. Furthermore, they were told just for him. "That was one of my principal pastimes all through the fifties, just sitting listening to their marvelous stories. It really entertained me—much more than any theatre or film or any form of public entertainment" (Tape, LDS).

He decided to take down, word by word, some of Yacoubi's stories and then translate them from the Moghrebi. The results soon appeared in *Evergreen Review* and other small journals. Bowles's lifetime interest in literary translation had thus taken an important new direction.[1]

In 1955, the year he completed and published *The Spider's House*, Bowles bought a tape recorder and set to work recording Yacoubi in earnest. As it turned out, Yacoubi became only the first in a procession of such young men, all equally adept at telling "invented" tales, all anxious to tell them into Bowles's machine. Of these, the most prolific has been Mohammed Mrabet, from whose narrations Bowles has translated and published two novels and two collections of stories, as well as numerous separate pieces. The most interesting of the storytellers has been Larbi Layachi, whom Bowles met in 1960. "A few anecdotes he told about his life impressed me deeply, not with their unusual content, but because of the way in which he recounted them. His rhetorical sense was extraordinary; he knew exactly which nuances and details to include in order to make a tale complete and convincing" (WS, p. 349). Under the nom de plume of Driss ben Hamed Charhadi, Larbi Layachi has dictated the memorable, autobiographical *A Life Full of Holes* (New York: Grove, 1964), the first Moghrebi "novel." There are two striking facts about all of these translations: Bowles converses with the storytellers in Spanish, but the stories are taped in, and translated from, the Moghrebi. And all the successful storytellers have been illiterate. "I'm inclined to believe that illiteracy is a prerequisite. The readers and writers I've tested have lost the necessary immediacy of contact with the material. They seem less in touch with both their memory and their imagination than the illiterates" (HRC: Note to Ryan).

Translation has perceptibly affected Bowles's own fiction, particularly the length of sentences. He feels that the pretranslation stories do not read aloud as well as those written later. And the later style has been influenced by the translations, "so much so that people get them all mixed up" (Tape, LDS). "Some think the translations are actually my own inventions, and others think the stories I invented are really folk tales" (TLS, PB to LDS, 16 Feb. 1973). This is particularly true of "The Hyena" and "The Garden," which in their brevity and subject matter have the strongest affinities to the translations. Perhaps to clarify his relationship to these Moghrebi tapes, Bowles has appeared on the title page of these more recent translations not only as "translator" but as "editor." And indeed he has had a formalistic effect upon these narratives.[2]

The experience with this younger generation of storytellers has also led Bowles to examine the power and implications of hemp. Earlier he had used majoun to provide the necessary images for Port's death in *The Sheltering Sky*, but until 1955 he had smoked kif only casually and without inhaling. In those days, hemp had for him been effective only as majoun. In the Moghrebi translations, however, kif was not only frequently the story's subject, *m'hashish* was invariably the state of the storyteller. Indeed at no time would one of these young storytellers attempt to narrate a tale until he had smoked kif and allowed its power to affect his consciousness. Mrabet's own explanation is characteristic:

> God gave me a brain that can invent stories. And I feed it with kif. When I drank alcohol I couldn't tell stories. When I gave up drinking and changed to kif, I began to tell stories again. . . . I smoke a little, shut my eyes, and then I begin to see everything. . . . If I tell one, before I've finished telling it I have an-

other in my head. It's like a chain. Give me twenty or thirty pipes of kif and let me lie under a tree or sit looking at the ocean, or just be in the house, looking at a plant growing in a flowerpot, or at one coal in the fire. Whatever is there opens up and changes while I'm watching it. An empty room can fill up with wonderful things, or terrible things. And the story comes from the things.[3]

When a child, Bowles wrote *An Opera in Nine Chapters*; his hero was an opium trafficker who had two wives. That appears to have been his earliest announced interest in narcotics as a way of dealing with life. The principal drug encountered in his youth was, of course, alcohol. Because he associated it with his troublesome parents and their noisy friends, he disliked it; and when he began to experiment with potions to alter the conscious personality, he was willing to try almost anything else first. At the University of Virginia, that meant sniffing ether; in Curaçao, smoking marijuana; in Tangier, eating majoun. But nothing seemed efficacious. Nor did experiments with hypnosis sufficiently detach him from his consciousness.

The year that he bought a tape recorder and set to work in his new role as Moghrebi translator, he turned to kif; now for the first time he began inhaling its smoke and investigating its function. Kif, used both as aesthetic pleasure and as an aid to composition, inevitably modified some of his notions—but less than one might assume. He had always felt that his writing had been an excursion into the unconscious. And he had always said that he could never argue effectively for any philosophical position, since that necessitated planning. The Baudelaire epigraph for "The Hours after Noon" had reassured him of the integrated unconscious; and clearly the effective pre-kif stories bring out philosophical attitudes which, in the corpus of his work, have consistency. *The Spider's House* dramatized Bowles's sympathy with the *status quo ante* the political disturbances of 1953. He now regarded forays into hashish as consistent with his politics: "It is to be expected that there should be a close relationship between the culture of a given society and the means used by its members to achieve release and euphoria. For Judaism and Christianity the means has always been alcohol; for Islam it has been hashish. The first is dynamic in its effects, the other static. If a nation wishes, however mistakenly, to Westernize itself, first let it give up hashish. The rest will follow, more or less as a matter of course" (HAG, p. 86).

Kif also helped him significantly, he thought, in the creative act. One cannot smoke and then expect to begin literary work. "It's the starting that gets hard, once you're smoking" (Tape, LDS). However, if one is already working and working well, a little kif can make him work "better" and prolong creative energy. Bowles emphasizes that no two people react similarly to hemp (and for some, the drug can have terrifying effects),[4] but he believes that for him it has been an unfailing aid, distorting perceptions only slightly. "What happens, really, is that you take things differently. They mean something different to you. It's not that they look different exactly, although if you have enough you can get into a state where you actually see them differently." Most important: to the author needing inspiration, kif can give the detonating vision for a story. "You can have total recall, if you want to have it" (Tape, LDS).

Majoun, on the other hand, has "nothing to do with the actual work. It's too strong. You have to give yourself up to it entirely and let it carry you where it will—learn how to use it, you know. You can't do anything for eight hours or something like that afterwards." But no matter what part of the cannabis that is consumed, and no matter in what form or intensity, "Whatever kif or any drug gives you is not determined by the kif itself. The kif is simply the key which opens a door to some particular chamber of the brain that lets whatever was in there out. It doesn't put anything in. It doesn't supply the matter. It liberates whatever's in, that's all" (Tape, LDS).

In the first few years of his kif episodes, Bowles was not always convinced of the propriety of insights so artificially produced. In a small green notebook that he carried with him from Ceylon to Kenya in 1957, he sketched the beginning of a novel: "The scene is the giant millpond which is the Indian Ocean in the breathless month before the monsoons break." He didn't go beyond some opening philosophical statements (such as he had used to get into "Pages from Cold Point"), but a portion of those speculations seems relevant to this discussion:

> I was thinking tonight of the necessity for understanding thoroughly that both chaos and order are incomplete concepts, reflecting passing emotional states, rather than any ultimate reality. . . . I suppose this is why religious dogma is so useful. A handy rule-of-thumb which makes identification of the self with the cosmos possible at any desired moment. But then isn't the identification rather like the sleep given by sedatives or the ecstasy induced by drugs? Isn't it better to achieve it naturally, even though it be more difficult? (HRC)

We do well not to forget that final sentence, when we consider the quality of these final works. Nor should we disregard the attitude of Jane Bowles, whose one experience with majoun resulted in an overdose: "from that day on she remained an implacable enemy of all forms of cannabis" (WS, p. 286). Bowles thought her attitude unreasonable; but he also thought it worth recording.

Bowles has never been interested in character as character. A notebook contains a draft of a letter he proposed sending a critic who had seen similarities between Bowles's work and that of the Southern Gothic school: "If it were only possible I should write without using people at all. This is an important point. Inasfar as it is practicable, I try to dispense with 'characters' entirely because they obstruct the view, and the reason they get in my way is that they don't interest me" (HRC). The essential quality of the kif story, therefore, harmonized with his own aesthetic, for it "is an endless, proliferated tale of intrigue and fantasy in which the unexpected turns of the narrative line play a far more decisive role than the development of character or plot." [5] In 1960–62, a group of his stories demonstrated this proposition.

On 16 October 1961, Allen Ginsberg, en route to India, wrote Bowles that Lawrence Ferlinghetti of City Lights Books was planning a new series of books; did Bowles have anything available? Bowles had recently published in some small magazines "A Friend of the World," "He of the Assembly," and "Merkala Beach" —three stories which shared a thematic interest in kif. On 29 November Ginsberg urged Bowles to contact Ferlinghetti: "maybe 3 kif stories be just right size for a pocket paperback. . . . I'm not sure, but certainly no harm contacting him, he be glad you're available to dance" (HRC). Bowles took Ginsberg's advice, and on 19 December 1961 Ferlinghetti replied that he "would be very interested in publishing three such smoking stories by yourself. THREE KIF STORIES ought to be a good title. Or perhaps THREE HASHISH STORIES would be more comprehensible for general consumption?" (HRC). Bowles agreed to prepare typescripts of the three tales ("I've got to copy them from the magazines") but asked Ferlinghetti to suppress all mention of Morocco itself: "Anyone who knows the region can infer from reading the stories that the country is Morocco, but that's not the same as using the word. . . . Moroccan diplomats take offence easily." Furthermore: "Do you object to THREE TALES OF KIF? Hashish doesn't come into them at all. They are not all equally concerned with the world of kif, but kif-smoking plays a decisive part in all of them" (HRC). There was further correspondence about an appropriate title; and then on 19 January 1962, Ferlinghetti exulted over the concluding line in "He of the Assembly" that Bowles had pointed out to him: "That new title is perfect—great— *A HUNDRED CAMELS IN THE COURTYARD*" (HRC). On 2 February Ferlinghetti acknowledged receipt of the "complete manuscreed and agree with you on all particulars, including use of your title, The Tale of Lahcen and Idir, for one of the stories, altho I do think this is the weakest title of the lot" (HRC). (That was Bowles's new title for "Merkala Beach." Ferlinghetti later urged retitling the story "Bird with Ring," but Bowles refused.) And then, that same February, before the book went to press, Bowles quickly wrote a fourth tale, "The Wind at Beni Midar." On 10 September 1962, Allen Ginsberg praised the just-published book: "you seem to have got the whole structure & exfoliation of a kif subjectivity episode all plotted out in detail in a story; that's more than I can keep track of in my own head" (HRC). Appropriately, the photo of Bowles that appears on the book's back cover had been taken by Ginsberg.

Bowles himself wrote the cover's blurb: "These are four tales of contemporary life in a land where cannabis, rather than alcohol, customarily provides a way out of the phenomenological world. . . . For all of them [the characters] the kif-pipe is the means to attaining a state of communication not only with others, but above all with themselves." The assumption of his aesthetic remained; only the methodology was different. But, as we shall see, that methodology had painful consequences and revealed the mind not always liberated but frequently tormented, as that "state of communication" occasionally became paranoid.

Of the four tales, "The Story of Lahcen and Idir" is most like a Moroccan fable. And though Bowles placed it third in his collection, it best establishes the distinction between kif and alcohol and dramatizes Bowles's attitude: "it's assumed, more or less, that the average person—man—doesn't live his life without a kind of psychedelic aid, one sort or another; [in Morocco] they take different things besides kif—herbs. . . . There's a belief in Morocco that the kif smoker always outwits the drinker—that alcohol makes a loser rather than a winner, whereas a kif smoker is clever and has his wits about him and can always win in any given situation." Moroccans may not insist that kif sharpens the brain, but they are convinced that it does not dull perception "the way alcohol does" (Tape, LDS). The Koran warns against befuddlement of the mind, but it does not mention herbs. These stories repeatedly emphasize that opposition to kif comes not from religious injunctions but from a government intent on bringing Morocco into the twentieth century. The present regime believes that the traditional toleration of the herbs was merely colonial decadence.

Bowles has always had unusual interest in magic and medicaments, relishing "the idea that in the night, all around me in my sleep [in Morocco], sorcery is burrowing its invisible tunnels in every direction, from thousands of senders to thousands of unsuspecting recipients.

Spells are being cast, poison is running its course; souls are being dispossessed of parasitic pseudo-consciousnesses that lurk in the unguarded recesses of the mind" (WS, p. 369). Both "A Friend of the World" and "The Wind at Beni Midar" build from this fascination. The former treats the subject lightly, depicting a Moroccan who has sufficient wit to play upon the psychological fears of his opponents. The latter story is based, however, upon religious and tribal beliefs, about which scant humor seems possible. The second story was written not only as the counterbalance; it grew out of material first developed for, and then deleted from, "A Friend of the World."

The published "A Friend of the World" tells how a young Moroccan, Salam, finds a kitten whom he innocently names "Mimi." Because in the Jewish quarter where he lives there also lives a young girl named Mimi, his kitten's name becomes regarded as an insult. The kitten is killed (we assume by the girl's mother), and Salam plots his revenge: make her believe that he has employed an old woman to cast a spell upon the child. When the child Mimi has an accident—nothing to do with spells or witchcraft—a policeman is asked to intervene. Eventually all complications are cleared away, and little harm is done anyone, except to the policeman. By a ruse he is transferred to a desert post because Salam feared that the policeman, having become consciously aware of Salam's existence, would inevitably arrest him for possessing kif.

At first Bowles titled his story "A Friend of the World and the Wrong Mimi." "A Friend of the World" appears, as a phrase, twice in the published tale, but not in the original manuscript. The story now has Salam state that "I'm a friend of the world. . . . A clean heart is better than everything" (TOF, p. 84); the manuscript did not reach that conclusion. Instead, it defined Salam's friendly nature in Tangier each month . . . [when] he went off and spent a few drunken nights and earned a few thousand francs to buy the next month's staples with. Once in a while he was very lucky, and got taken on a trip to Europe, and was bought a new suit and everything to go with it. When he came back, he always ended by selling whatever clothes he had collected. . . . He had started out with one lady on Tuesdays and Fridays, but this meant that he had to live in Tangier, and after a few months of paying for him she had put an end to it. But through her he had met another English lady who suggested they spend Saturdays and Sundays together at her apartment. He accepted the suggestion. When the first lady saw what had happened she took him back for Tuesdays and Fridays. In this way, with an added lady thrown in occasionally from a chance meeting in a bar, Salam managed to make enough in the one week each month for him and Bou Ralem to live. (HRC)

All of the *Hundred Camels* stories reduce friendship to trade and the exchange of services. Within another year or two, however, "The Time of Friendship" would return to "friendship" its historic nobility.

In his original plot, Bowles had Salam acquire a replacement kitten. (" 'This one's going to have a Moslem name,' said Salam. 'I don't want any more trouble.' He named the kitten Farid.") That second cat, and the coincidence of again a duplicated name, was to have created a conflict within the policeman, a rational man who does not willingly subscribe to all the old talk of spells and incantations. "When he went home he asked his wife if it were possible to make magic by using cats. 'Where did you hear such a thing?' she asked him. He told her. 'Who knows what Jews do?' she said. 'No, the woman said it was a Moslem.' 'I never heard of using cats,' said his wife. 'But it might work' " (HRC).

After the policeman had gone to see the Jewish woman, he heard a voice calling "Farid!"

He turned his head and saw a man looking down at him from the terrace. The man was a Moslem, and he was laughing. The policeman was annoyed, because he felt the man was laughing at him, but he did not want to speak to him. He walked back to the comisaría. When he got home that night his wife was weeping because the youngest child, Farid, had just burned his hand on the stove. The policeman did not believe in magic, but while he ate his dinner he thought about it. He had heard the man call the name Farid. (HRC)

The coincidence, as well as its implications that troubled the rational man, were canceled in the manuscript. But the situation—one not wishing to believe in magic becomes compelled, against his will and through ocular proof, to accept that belief—became the basis of the corollary story, "The Wind at Beni Midar."

Because he knew what effect "The Wind at Beni Midar" must produce—what further statement it must make about the efficacy of kif—Bowles first wrote several hundred words of notes and plot summary, associating the herb with spells and the primitive faith of country Berbers (as distinguished from the more orthodox Moslem faith of townspeople). In 1951, when Bowles had been in Xauen completing *Let It Come Down*, he had gone to a café one evening to hear some native music. A man came in, began to dance, and then went into a trance: moving and moaning ritualistically he slashed himself formally, first on his arms—which he wiped over himself to paint his face—and then on the backs of his legs. Covered in blood, he sank with a beatific expression into unconsciousness—all this to the accompaniment of native music whose rhythms gradually moderated. After an interval in which they drank tea and smoked kif, the musicians resumed their playing; the new tempo restored the dancer to consciousness. He arose, kissed each of them on the forehead, paid them some money, drank his tea, and left the café, a happy man. He was a Djilali, a member of a Moslem brotherhood now composed largely of Berbers. Bowles found the experience so remarkable that he worked it into the conclusion of his novel, finding for Dyar a personal catharsis in witnessing the act: "The mutilation was being done for him, to him; it was his own blood that spattered onto the drums and made the floor slippery. In a world which had not yet been muddied by the discovery of thought, there was this certainty, as solid as a boulder, as real as the beating of his heart, that the man was dancing to purify all who watched" (LICD, p. 287).

In 1955, the year he began his kif experiences, Bowles wrote again about the Djilala, this time in his own voice: "To me these spectacles are filled with great beauty, because their obvious purpose is to prove the power of the spirit over the flesh" (HAG, pp. 27–28). The city dwellers, bent on moving Morocco into the twentieth century, are "violent in their denunciation of the cults," probably because "most of them are only one generation removed from them themselves; knowing the official attitude toward such things, they feel a certain guilt at being even that much involved with them" (HAG, pp. 28–29). The reflex conditioned in childhood seems, however, to be inescapable. Bowles had a friend, for example, whose

> earliest memories were of being strapped to his mother's back while she, dancing with the others, attained a state of trance. The two indispensable exterior agents . . . were drums and djaoui [a resinous

substance]. By the time the boy was four or five years old, he already had a built-in mechanism, an infallible guarantee of being able to reach the trance state very swiftly in the presence of the proper stimulus . . . with the result that now as a man in his mid-twenties, although he is at liberty to accept or refuse the effect of the specific drum rhythms, he is entirely at the mercy of a pinch of burning djaoui. (HAG, p. 30)

Many of those attitudes Bowles adapted for "The Wind at Beni Midar." The story was to have been about a soldier, Benahmed, who on a Sunday in a kif reverie eats some cactus fruit and loses a borrowed pistol. A portion of Bowles's plot outline reads: "The captain watches him over a period of time, decides for one reason or another that he smokes kif, and having been a smoker himself, reconstructs the . . . [movements] of Benahmed as he walks along same road. Discovers chumbos, guesses that Benahmed has eaten them, and thus finds the pistol under the pile of rotten parings. The captain, with bourgeois contempt for the superstitions of the country people, amuses himself with Benahmed by pretending that he can burn djaoui and having gone into a trance then learn where the pistol is. Benahmed scoffs at the idea, with the violence that comes from his desire to escape from the world of the Djilala." After the captain has produced the gun, Benahmed "goes out of barracks to the village and smokes kif, fixing blame for his state of nervousness and tension on the captain, as if it were the captain who were profiting by his state of subjection to the powers of djaoui. This idea is the one that finally prompts Benahmed to take action." Benahmed buys a potion and "Captain loses use of right hand. Happiness this news causes Benahmed, since thus he knows Allah is on his side, since had the captain been innocent, the poison would not have worked. He assuages his sense of guilt thus, at the same time lessening his fear of outside powers by remembering that his magic was stronger than the captain's" (HRC).

Bowles made a note to "Invent incident at beginning which can bring out B's dislike of Djilala, his desire to escape into an unpostulated world of relative rationality." When he later rechristened his protagonist Driss, replaced the pistol with a rifle, and reduced the captain to a corporal—thereby making more plausible the friendship between the two soldiers—Bowles remarked: "Driss's vengeance is motivated by resentment at being proven wrong, at therefore having to remain imprisoned in the irrational world. Consciously mortified by laughter, resentful at having been mocked, frightened at having been a victim of supernatural power, vindictive because the corporal has dared to use magic at his expense. (If magic works that well, I'll use it, too.)" (HRC).

Bowles himself has no doubts about the potions of Morocco: "Apothecary shops also sell ingredients—that isn't medicine, that's something else. That's for manipulation (what we used to call 'magic' when we didn't believe it existed). But of course when one comes here one realizes it certainly does exist. It's part of the fabric of everyday life. And it *works!*" (*Paul Bowles in the Land of the Jumblies*). His own belief in *tseuheur*—defined by him as "the theory and practice of black magic" —has deepened since the mid-fifties. Perhaps kif itself is merely another demonstration of the magic of herbs. When Bowles first sketched his ideas for "The Wind at Beni Midar," he wanted to intensify Driss's response to magic by making him "mejdoub. This was a dark secret that not all the brothers and sisters knew. She [his sister] knew because she had carried him on her back while she played, and she had seen him the first time the smoke of the djaoui had carried him away. One night many years ago the family had gone to an amara in the mountains. They sat in a tent with the drums beating just outside, and an old man came in swinging a pot. Blue smoke came out of it" (HRC). The completed story deletes that explanation for Driss's response. Instead it suggests that the belief in black magic is atavistic and that the civilized man's resistance to belief is easily overcome.

Driss dislikes the Djilala. "They did not dance because they wanted to dance, and it was this that made him angry and ashamed. It seemed to him that the world should be made in such a way that a man is free to dance or not as he feels. A Djilali can do only what the music tells him to do." Driss has hope, but little confidence, that the government will change all this. When he is told that he must turn to these same Djilala for help, he is mortified. But the cabran assures him that "When the Djilali is drinking his own blood he has power. What you have to do is ask him to make the *djinn* bring me the gun. I'm going to sit in my room and burn *djaoui*." The return of the gun convinces Driss. "It was the first time he had had anything to do with a *djinn* or an *affrit*. Now he had entered into their world. It was a dangerous world." So powerful is the resurrection of his suppressed faith, that even when he overhears the cabran and learns that all has been a hoax, he is not dissuaded. "It was the cabran's fault that the *djinn* had been called, and now in front of his superior officers he was pretending that he had had nothing to do with it," he thinks. Kif helps along these beliefs and encourages his further investment in sorcery. When he poisons the cabran's drink, "Then he was sure that the cabran's soul had been torn out of his body and that the power was truly broken. In his head he made a prayer of thanks to

Allah." To Driss, kif has brought neither enlightenment nor the innocence of reverie. It has strengthened his paranoia and returned him to a primitivism which Bowles has long admired: a world with its own logic, where causes are assignable to spells and incantations and not to the games played by the individual intelligence.

When there is alteration of the mind, either through disease or drugs, delusions masquerade as truth. Whether it is the illness of Port, the madness of Dyar, or the paranoia of Driss, the pursuit of the obliteration of consciousness has social implications. Both Norton and Port have fractured the world and made an individual escape; where harm is done it is done primarily to themselves. But the escapes provided by kif—as dramatized in Bowles's stories—are bought at the destruction of others: Thami is murdered, the cabran is destroyed. In the years since he wrote *A Hundred Camels in the Courtyard*, Bowles has become somewhat less enthusiastic an admirer of indulgence: "I'm all in favor of the Dionysian stance, you know. But apparently you can't keep it up and not be mindless. Well, I'm not in favor of mindlessness simply because it's impossible to keep parliamentary procedure with mindlessness. Any group that adjures rationality makes itself a useful tool for any conspiratorial group" (*Paul Bowles in the Land of the Jumblies*). Kif, which had begun for him as the guarantee of the *status quo*, seemingly makes possible a newer and more heinous kind of totalitarian imposition.

All early drafts of "The Wind at Beni Midar" labeled it merely "At Beni Midar." But a recurrent theme in all of these kif tales is man's relationship to nature, another kind of magic: "certain areas of the earth's surface contained more magic than others," Bowles believed. He defined magic as "a secret connection between the world of nature and the consciousness of man, a hidden but direct passage which bypassed the mind. (The operative word here is 'direct,' because in this case it was equivalent to 'visceral.')" (WS, p. 125). Throughout these stories, nature manifests itself as the wind, particularly the wind of change. In the best of the four stories, "He of the Assembly," the protagonist, deep in his kif reverie, listens to the wind in the telephone wires. There is the music that stimulates fantasy; there is the symbol of modernity that blows across the land and threatens its customs and beliefs.

In his autobiography, Bowles accounted for the existence of these kif stories as solutions to puzzles posed for himself: "Let us say that I started with four disparate fragments—anecdotes, quotations, or simple clauses deprived of context—gleaned from separate sources and involving, if anything, entirely different sets of characters. The task was to . . . make all four of the original elements equally supportive of the resulting construction. . . . By using kif-inspired motivations, the arbitrary could be made to seem natural, the diverse elements could be fused, and several people would automatically become one" (WS, p. 347).

In *The Spider's House*, the novelist Stenham was accustomed to native stories as part of the entertainment at Si Jaffar's. But he "found it impossible to follow these stories; he understood the words, but he never got the point"; invariably he hoped for "some further clue which might connect all the parts." Si Jaffar conceded that "Some of our stories are very difficult. Even the people from Rabat and Casablanca often must have them explained, because the stories are meant only for the people of Fez. But that's what gives them their perfume. They wouldn't be amusing if everyone could follow them" (SH, pp. 221–22). The best of Bowles's four kif tales shows him determined both to get the point and to connect all the parts.

"He of the Assembly" grew from Bowles's friendship with Boujemaa, a young Moroccan whose name means, literally, He of the Assembly. "He's a crazy man in Marrakech who gives you these little fragments. And you say, 'But what does it mean?' And then he just smiles. He never will tell you anything" (Tape, LDS).[6] In the Djemaa el Fna, Boujemaa told Bowles: "The eye wants to sleep, but the head is no mattress," and "The sky trembles and the earth is afraid, and the two eyes are not brothers." "By giving me these fragmentary sentences he aroused my curiosity to such a point that I had to explain it for myself by writing a story about it. It's explained to my satisfaction—my own, that's all. It's a story. It doesn't mean anything beyond what happens" (Tape, LDS). But even "what happens" is not easily deciphered in the printed account. Although Christopher Isherwood finds it quintessential Bowles—indeed, the finest of all his stories—for others of his admirers it has had a troubling opacity.

Bowles submitted "He of the Assembly" to the *London Magazine*, but John Lehmann rejected the story "with great regret," calling it interesting but a failure: "The dope-dream atmosphere seems to me to become merely a confusion, and I fear that too many readers will give up bewildered before they have got half-way" (HRC: TLS, 26 Feb. 1960). The story appeared later that year in *Big Table*.

Bowles admires Larbi Layachi's narrative ability. "To anyone understanding Moghrebi, Charhadi's tapes are a pleasure to listen to: spacing of words, inflections of the voice in passages reporting conversation, and unexpected means of supplying emphasis" (HRC), he noted around 1960. And that is also what his own voice gives to "He of the Assembly." "I've discovered that it makes sense when I read it aloud. To me it makes more sense, even. When I read it on the paper I can see that it lacks a certain dimension that it needs. It lacks air because of the way so many things are crammed into one paragraph each time. . . . Actually, it has to be read aloud. I've discovered that. That's one that really *needs* to be read aloud" (Tape, LDS). But his taping of "He of the Assembly" is not publicly available, and the story's meaning must be deciphered from its typography.

The published form of it "is crazy," Bowles admits. "It's built on four levels—it's in seven paragraphs, the story. Level 1 is the same as level 7; 2 is the same as 6, 3 is the same as 5, and 4 is a kind of interior monologue which is told in the first person, which is the crucial part, which is the center—or the top, if you like—of the pyramid" (Tape, LDS). When he began working with Boujemaa's fragments, he had not envisioned so balanced a construction. The holograph draft's brief second paragraph, for example, contrasted tourists with natives— those who drink alcohol with those who smoke kif. A couple rides in a carriage: "They were always drunk, because they were afraid to see what the world would look like if they were not drunk. They travelled nearly all the time, but they did not see the world" (HRC), and we hear something of their quarrelsome conversation. In the published version—which, like all these kif stories, depicts only a Moslem world—that intrusive couple disappears into "the last carriage [that] went by, taking the last tourists down the road beside the ramparts to their rooms in the Mamounia."

Having devised his seven-paragraph structure, Bowles did not worry unduly about typographical aids within the paragraph. He used quotation marks sparingly. Speakers change, and we move uncertainly between their meditations and their spoken thoughts. When Bowles made his final typescript, he marked extra wide spacing between the first and second of his seven paragraphs— and this spacing is maintained in all of his collections that include this work. But otherwise, caesuras and breaks must be decided upon by the reader. Reading this story is akin to reading and phrasing music. If the reader is willing to make the effort at interpretation, he will find "He of the Assembly" peculiarly satisfying.

Perhaps because of the nature of the detonating material for this story, Bowles made great use throughout it of other sayings and proverbs. These range from the casual ambiguity, "It ends that way" (which mortises together paragraphs 5 and 6) to a variant on the old Americanism, "a jewel in my crown" (which parallels paragraphs 3 and 7). Unlike the two cryptic remarks of Boujemaa (which help join paragraphs 1 and 2 to 6 and 7), one saying is used only once—at the very end. It is the remark that Bowles had heard often around Marrakech and occasionally in Tangier: "A pipe of kif before breakfast gives a man the strength of a hundred camels in the courtyard." [7] Even though "He of the Assembly" has been set in the twilight world of the kif fantasy, that proverb, with its almost didactic directness, brings us abruptly into a world of light. Bowles was determined that the surreality of Boujemaa's remarks should have a logical radiance—much the same way that Cocteau in *Orphée* made the senselessness of Apollinaire's *"L'oiseau chante avec ses doigts"* sensible. When a young man, Bowles wished not to impose structure upon his resurrected unconscious—thus his cryptic and hermetic poetry. It is remarkable that in the finest of his kif stories he determined that events must have perceptible causes. The twilight world was no longer to be mindless.

We see this particularly in Bowles's new attitude toward the delusions produced by cannabis. When He of the Assembly smokes in the Café of the Two Bridges, he knows rationally that he is safe: no policeman dares to enter a café owned by the Sultan's sister. But as he inhales smoke from his *sebsi*, his mind plays with the fantasy of entrapment. " 'If I got up and ran down the street,' he thought, 'a policeman would follow me and call to me to stop.' " So begins for him a concatenation of images and events, but each detail and incident that comes to his consciousness gives him pause. Why that reaction to his own conjuration? He requires that all make sense to himself, just as Bowles himself would build order from Boujemaa's fragments. In this light, "He of the Assembly" is not merely the description of a young kif smoker, it is another portrait of the artist.

He of the Assembly recognized that he "was in a café where no policeman could come, and he wanted to go away to a kif world where the police were chasing him. 'This is the way we are now,' he thought. 'We work backwards. If we have something good, we look for something bad instead. . . . The world is too good. We can only work forward if we make it bad again first.' This made him sad, so he stopped thinking, and filled his *sebsi*." Kif creates, therefore, the *necessary* delusion. Bowles once explained to a critic that the violence and persecution in his work was not a decorative Gothicism:

> your assumption that a novel ought to contain character analysis and a sense of social reality is pretty arbitrary. There is a fairly large section of the reading public for which reading performs a kind of therapy. What you call "the terrible" is what I should call merely a counter-irritant to the vague sense of anguish of which this public is conscious. . . . What they want is escape literature in reverse. The more unpleasant the experience of reading, the less painful the return to the familiar disgust with life. It's a game of "Let's pretend life is an unmitigated nightmare and we're all monsters"; they must know per-

fectly well that at its worst the experience of living can scarcely be more than a rather pale facsimile of a nightmare. (HRC)

In the story, the alliance of Ben Tajah and He of the Assembly commences in mutual need. Ben Tajah has found in the Djemaa el Fna an envelope bearing his name. He opens it inside the Café of the Two Bridges and reads: "The sky trembles and the earth is afraid, and the two eyes are not brothers." Ben Tajah thinks it the work of Satan, and he is troubled. Also in the café is He of the Assembly; he is deep in a paranoid kif reverie that has transported him out of the café until he is chased by the police, "And I'd be running through the streets looking for a place to hide." He finds an open door, passes into a kitchen where there is an old woman stirring a big kettle of soup. "If you're trying to get away, my boy, I can help you. Jump into the soupkettle." [8] And thus, like Alice plunging into the rabbit hole, he climbs down a ladder into the kettle. " 'Until the other world!' he shouted." He gets into a rowboat and rows off into the steaming dark. "He was worried about the old woman, and he thought he must find a way to help her."

Then, somehow delivered from the soupkettle, he sees Ben Tajah in the café, and he thinks: "That man has no one in the world." (A deleted line had asked: "If you have no one in the world, is there any world?") He of the Assembly is seventeen but he has no one either, other than his aunt. Later that evening, when the two encounter each other unexpectedly outside Ben Tajah's door, He of the Assembly wonders if he could not share the old man's life. The young man, *m'hashish*, cannot go to his aunt; and how many more nights can he raise money to pay for a place to sleep? Each is plagued by his own concerns: Ben Tajah questions that the letter, which he now cannot find, really existed; and if it did, what does it mean? He of the Assembly is convinced that he was indeed in a soupkettle, but how did he escape from it and from the police? Each promises to set the other's mind at rest. Bowles's plot notes for paragraph 7 read:

> kif gives out in Café. H of A. asks Ben Tajah to explain to him how he could have climbed into the soupkettle and got back out. B. T. understood that the effect of the kif was growing less. But he saw that it had not really gone, or H of A would not have asked the question, and he said: "Wait until tomorrow for the answer to that question." H of A. thought this was an invitation to spend the night. It was late and he was tired. "Good," he said, and he took off his djellaba and lay down to sleep. (HRC)

Is there a sexual relationship implied by this act? "In the mind of He of the Assembly there is" (Tape, LDS), says Bowles. It is not in Ben Tajah's mind. He of the Assembly wants their relationship based on trust. But he knows that the old man worries about the alleged letter, and thus the young man lies to him and says that the perplexing lines are from a song.

> Ben Tajah clapped his hands together hard. "A song!" he cried. "I must have heard it on the radio." He of the Assembly shrugged. "They play it sometimes," he said. "I've made him happy," he thought. "But I won't ever tell him another lie. That's the only one. What I'm going to do now is not the same as lying."

What he does now is take off his djellaba and get into Ben Tajah's bed. Surprised, Ben Tajah "meant to stay awake, but he went to sleep because he was not used to smoking kif." When He of the Assembly discovers that Ben Tajah is not feigning sleep or indifference, he becomes angry. He gets up, dresses silently, and takes all of Ben Tajah's money. It was in the description of this act that Bowles inserted in his typescript an incident that profoundly altered the concluding effect of the story.

Throughout "He of the Assembly" we are not certain that Ben Tajah's letter really existed. After all, he is not a young man and he has just returned from Fez on a two-day, exhausting bus trip. Perhaps the letter was as delusional as the kif dreams in the café. At the moment He of the Assembly takes Ben Tajah's money, however, Bowles added sentences to show that there was indeed a letter and that He of the Assembly found it tucked among the banknotes. A candle burned beside the bed. "He of the Assembly held the paper above the flame and burned it, and then he burned the envelope. He blew the black paper-ashes across the floor."

Seemingly, Ben Tajah has kept none of his agreements with the young man; but the old man knows that when the kif wears out, the questions about the soup-kettle will disappear. He of the Assembly, however, has not yet returned to such clear-headedness, and he knows only that he must have money to buy more kif—since kif, which got him into the soupkettle, may bring an explanation for his escape. The innocence of his delusion, as well as the generosity of his final act, distinguishes him as more than merely a predatory young man from the streets. For the first time in a Bowles short story, the crossgenerational relationship is one of compensatory kindness. Friendship is no longer pernicious barter and exchange, and it carries no sexual price. How far indeed is Ben Tajah's bed in Marrakech from Norton's at Cold Point.

In the winter of 1947–48, while working on *The Sheltering Sky*, Bowles traveled south into Algeria; the journey supplied not only the immediacy of details woven daily into the work-in-progress, but also the story of the Tabelbala leather workers who later made their way into "The Delicate Prey." The happiest product of his excursion, however, came nearly fifteen years later when its memory generated "The Time of Friendship," a novella which is the culmination of his feelings about North Africa.[9]

That 1947–48 winter he had

> continued by produce truck to Taghit, probably the most intensely poetic spot I had ever seen. The tiny hotel atop the rocks was run in conjunction with the military fort nearby. There was a solitary old servant who did everything; fortunately he had only one other guest besides me, an elderly Swiss lady who taught school in Zurich and spent her winters in the Sahara. She and I got on perfectly and took long walks together in the valley to the south. (WS, p. 282)

Bowles kept in touch with her for many years, for she made annual visits to Taghit. But he has not "heard from her, not since around '62, about the time I wrote the story. That Christmas she sent me a little Christmas tree—from Switzerland, not from the desert—and said that she hadn't been able to go back . . . and this put the idea in my head: 'the war's now keeping poor Fräulein from going to her favorite spot.' The Algerian War got it going in my head. So I wanted to write about it" (Tape, LDS). The letter from Switzerland had confirmed his prediction made seven years earlier: "the crucial Algerian struggle is to the 'fifties rather what the Spanish Civil War was to the 'thirties. Friendships break up as a result of bitter arguments. . . . But regardless of how the tragic episode terminates, no part of North Africa will again be the same sort of paradise for Europeans that it was during the past fifty years." [10] This novella is the elegy commemorating that loss.

The story tells of Fräulein Windling who has gone to an oasis near Taghit for many years (the manuscript says seven)—gone there ever since her "first sight of the desert and its people had been a transfiguring experience." She "believed firmly that each day she spent here increased the aggregate of her resistance." (The manuscript states that "She believed the white race to be a degenerate form of humanity; her desire was to become strong and stoical like the primitives of the oasis" [HRC].) There she lives a quiet hotel life; usually she is the only guest. She would play solitaire, write letters, and go for long walks through the river valley. (The manuscript reads: "It seemed to her that before she had come to this place she had been able to see the world only through books; now she felt that she perceived it directly" [HRC].) Sometimes when the wind blew fiercely and covered all other sounds, she "merely sat, watching the burnt-out logs as they fell to pieces before her eyes." [11]

The benefits of nature must now be repaid by attention to the natives: " 'A new generation requires a new technique if one is to establish contact,' she thought. 'It is for me to find it.' " It is found for her by a young boy who appears at the hotel one morning and stands looking through her open door. Gradually they make contact. "She would tell him to come in, and they would shake hands gravely, he afterward raising the backs of his fingers to his lips." She knows that if she asks his name he will not give the true one. But one day, when he is telling her "several legends involving the great Moslem king of long ago, whose name was Solomon," he says "And my name too is Slimane, the same as the king."

She tries to teach him to read, but it is hopeless; and the first year of their friendship concludes with her return to Switzerland late in March. She will now be able to entertain her pupils with new tales of desert life where, she pretends, "everything was made by the people themselves out of what the desert had to offer." Preferring to think of the desert as a "world of objects fashioned out of baked earth, woven grass, palmwood and animal skins," she cannot confess that the goathide water bags have been replaced by empty oil tins.

That second year "was probably her happiest season in the desert, that winter of comradeship when together they made the countless pilgrimages down the valley." "She told him about Jesus, Martin Luther and Garibaldi, taking care to keep Jesus distinct from the Moslem prophet Sidna Aissa." Only when she touched upon Islam would Slimane protest. "No, no, no, no! Nazarenes know nothing about Islam. Don't talk, madame, I beg you." (How unlike those No's of Port Moresby, the denial beneath that sheltering sky; here they assert belief.) That March when Fräulein Windling returns to Switzerland she recognizes, "Next year you'll be a man."

The third year the French are reluctant to renew her visa; and in her absence Slimane has tried, unsuccessfully, to run away. She cannot tell him her life in the oasis is ending: "If he, at least, still had the illusion of unbounded time lying ahead, he would somehow retain his sense of purity and innocence," she thinks. But the thoughts of the fourteen-year-old are now with his friends who are "killing the French like flies." Nevertheless their excursions continue. When they disagree about Jesus, she determines to construct a crèche for Christmas Eve. "She wanted only to suggest to him that the god with whom he was on such intimate terms was the god worshiped by the Nazarenes." Their outings decrease as she spends her time, hammering and sculpting in secret. She thinks of the photographs she will take "of the crèche and of Slimane looking at it"—the

evidence that innocence can be preserved and friendship fused through religion.

She had invited Slimane to dinner Christmas Eve at
the hotel; but so concerned is she about the crèche she
forgets to tell the hotelkeeper, who sends Slimane home:
"He wanted to come into the dining-room. . . . And
he knows it's forbidden at dinner time." Later Fräulein
Windling learns that Slimane has gone supperless,
walking around outside the hotel in the cold. When
Slimane is admitted to the dining-room and the crèche
is revealed, he thinks it has been brought from Switzerland—so cleverly has she disguised the native elements
from which it is made. But then she shows him how it
is assembled of almonds, tangerines, and dates, as well
as foil-wrapped candies. To Slimane, the crèche is food.
And when she returns with her camera, prepared to take
the long-planned photograph, she finds that all has become a shambles of sand, date stones, and "here and
there a carefully folded square of lavender or pink tin-
foil." That night as she lies in bed she reminds herself
that "food is not an adornment." Had she not invited
him to dinner? And was this not the only dinner offered? "It has been too much head and high ideals . . .
and not enough heart."

On Christmas Day the French close the desert to
civilians; she must leave immediately: "it's the end, and
the time of friendship is finished," she knows. Slimane
accompanies her to Colomb-Bechar; as they wait there
on the terrace of a café she gives him money for his
return ticket home. She says she will send a little more
from time to time. He thinks she is sad "because I ate
the food out of the picture. That was very bad. Forgive
me." Only then does she break down. Once aboard the
train, she receives from Slimane his address which another had written for him. As the train pulls out, "he
was running, until all at once there was no more plat-

form. She leaned far out, looking backward, waving."
And then she reads his address; it is not in the oasis but
in Colomb-Bechar. He has run away to become a soldier
and she, who has despised "everything military," has
been the unwitting agent of destruction. "She saw her
own crooked, despairing smile in the dark window-glass
beside her face."

Bowles's 1947–48 visit to Taghit helped with the
story's essential details: there had been "a little boy
named Suliman who used to come and see her—they
were great friends—she did actually make a crèche for
him, and that's about all. The rest of it's all my imagination, because I transposed it from '48 when it actually
happened to, say, ten years later, after the Algerian War
had been going a few years" (Tape, LDS). Bowles did
not model Fräulein Windling upon her prototype, but
he did retain her Swiss background ("She actually did
teach, at the Freiluftschüle in Bern") and build from
her attitude which had so impressed him: "She was in
love with the desert and the people. And she somehow
imagined that all Europeans were what she called
degueneres—she spoke very bad French—and that the
people who lived in the Sahara were healthy, natural, as
opposed to the degenerate Europeans" (Tape, LDS).

Considering what Bowles published, it is astonishing
how he began. Evidently he thought that only a woman
of forceful opinions could prosper in such privation. In
his first drafts he said: "she had once dressed up in men's
clothing, burnous and all, and ridden horseback with a
group of Moungara all the way to Sidi Moungari, where
she had spent the night outside the shrine, rolled in a
camel's blanket." "Whatever sympathy she withheld
from the women she more than made up for when it
came to the men. She could be found any time between
dawn and sunset in the marketplace, out on the dunes,
or down in the middle of the oasis, arguing with one

man or a group of men." The hotelkeeper "had to agree with the villagers that she was not like other Nazarenes, although he scoffed at their theory that she was at the mercy of a djinn" (HRC). But none of that would serve. Now she observes the natives, but it is the natural world she focuses upon, for it has brought her there. She lies in the sun, gathering its fading glow; and where there must be personal communion, she lives by writing letters. The French soldiers in the hotel interest her so little they no longer bother with pleasantries. Her admiration of the natives is an appreciation of type and not of individuals. She goes her solitary way and tries to accept, almost with Moslem passivity, whatever comes. But even in her resolute passivity she cannot easily accept separation from the oasis and her annual pilgrimage of personal restoration.

There is the paradox that she is the teacher, one committed to change. But she works only for the money that provides the escape to this primitive innocence. The force of change is itself doubly felt in this story: there is the political change, brought by the war; there is the natural development of the boy. At first, Bowles thought of Slimane as a ten-year-old, but by the earliest typescripts he is already twelve. At one time we were even to have seen him matured, for there had been planned a fourth season in the oasis:

When she first caught sight of Slimane, he was loping along in the sand under the tamarisk trees, and straightway she observed that the time had arrived: he had slipped over into being a man. It was natural, she thought wryly, for things to grow, but since growing seemed always to mean becoming uglier, she supposed that the state of maturity was intended by nature to be unattractive, in order to reinforce the beauty and desirability of youth.

There was difficulty in the Fräulein Windling–Slimane relationship, particularly with regard to the boy. Is he exceptional? Is he poetic? Or is he merely typical, the embodiment and personification of Fräulein Windling's admired primitivism? It is the problem of Amar all over again, though Slimane has none of Amar's religious wisdom or city background. That third winter, Slimane is fourteen, and there needs must be his emerging sexuality. How was it to be treated? Bowles experimented in his notebooks with a paragraph:

> He laid the palms of his two hands gently against her cheeks, and in that moment she saw him again as he had come along the road yesterday, and then she understood that he had begun to visit the Ouled Naïl girls at the bottom of the cliffs below the village.
>
> "Zoui-i-ina," he said under his breath, so low that she could scarcely hear him, although his face was almost touching hers, "*very* nice." His hands were still on her cheeks, but his eyes had turned aside and were looking beyond her. (HRC)

All this is canceled, and the published account retains a presexual ideality.

But no matter what his sexual innocence, Slimane nonetheless recognizes power. And just as she has attempted, quietly, to understand him, so has he accepted and understood her. The stories she has told him have helped foster his independence. Even her beloved Christ—was he not one who acts? "When Sidna Aissa has returned for forty days there will be no more Moslems and the world will end. Everything, the sky and the sun and the moon. And the wind too. Everything." Thus for him to act, is this not to make the teacher proud? Again we are confronted with the reversed intention of the well-meaning foreigner.

Fräulein Windling has contrasted the European with the North African, the mechanical with the natural. She has also contrasted Christianity with Islam. The fact that Christ has a role, an important one, in the Koran mystifies her. She calls it a Pyrrhic victory, and "its inconsistency embarrassed her." But Slimane sees the world as one, and his faith accommodates even the stranger in the oasis who has been a Nazarene and a friend. For what is friendship but acceptance? Friendship is not imposition, it is comprehension.

The train from Colomb-Bechar "began its long climb upwards over the plateau." That phrase ends the story, as the experience ends Fräulein Windling's life; for that train carries her into the inevitability of death. How can she survive permanent separation from her beloved oasis and its essential restorative power? But it is the death of Slimane that is now in her thoughts. Only by death can he become part of the land that has nourished them both. And only in death is his innocence made immutable. " 'If only death were absolutely certain in wartime,' she thought wryly, 'the waiting would would not be so painful.' " In the finest of his later works, Bowles thereby repudiates the philosophy of Norton and his meaningless immurement. Now that the dreaded bomb has fallen impersonally upon the native and the foreigner, there is no fragmentation; ironically there is only the unifying nobility that comes through love and friendship. Life becomes acceptance, for only acceptance bridges generations and the contrarieties of religion. A notebook entry for the story's end had read:

> explaining that desert gave meaning to F. W.'s life. She had always felt that life must be more profound and important than it appeared to her. The Sahara had proved her suspicions correct. . . . Now she knew that the mystery & beauty were not to be found

in the dark corners of the earth, but under the glaring face of the Absolute, in the desert. (HRC)

The mirror that Bowles held up to the nature of North Africa reflected many things, but always himself and its sun. The conclusion of his autobiography, *Without Stopping*, restates Valéry's epigram that had been epigraph to a portion of *The Sheltering Sky*: " 'Good-bye,' says the dying man to the mirror they hold in front of him. 'We won't be seeing each other any more.' " The autobiography had been such uncongenial labor (how could biographical facts recapture what had been his reality?) that he now appended to the Valéry remark, "Thank God!" But there speaks not the man whose writings illuminated North Africa and placed himself in the context of its glowing world. His fiction has always made plain that, for him, separation from North Africa is separation from self. His life has passed in reconciling self-awareness with the self's unconscious dreams. The inside/outside fusion that Gertrude Stein had labeled "entity" remains this artist's essential need. The extent to which he bridges the irreconcilable gives his fiction its special radiance.

Notes

Abbreviations

WORKS BY PAUL BOWLES

DP   *The Delicate Prey and Other Stories* (New York: Random House, 1950).

HAG   *Their Heads Are Green and Their Hands Are Blue* (New York: Random House, 1963).

HAN   *The Hours after Noon* (London: Heinemann, 1959).

LICD   *Let It Come Down* (New York: Random House, 1952).

SH   *The Spider's House* (New York: Random House, 1955).

SS   *The Sheltering Sky* (New York: New Directions, 1949).

TOF   *The Time of Friendship* (New York: Holt, Rinehart & Winston, 1967).

TOS   *The Thicket of Spring: Poems 1926–1969* (Los Angeles: Black Sparrow, 1972).

WS   *Without Stopping* (New York: Putnam's, 1972).

Y   *Yallah* (New York: McDowell, Obolensky, 1957).

OTHER ABBREVIATIONS

HRC   Paul Bowles Collection, Humanities Research Center, the University of Texas at Austin

PB   Paul Bowles

LDS   Lawrence D. Stewart

Yale   The Gertrude Stein Collection, the Beinecke Rare Book and Manuscript Library, Yale University Library

ALS   autograph letter signed

LS   letter signed

TL   typed letter, unsigned

TLS   typed letter signed

TS   typescript

1 First Light

1. Cf. John Hyde Preston, "A Conversation," *Atlantic Monthly* 156 (August 1935), 188–89, quoting Gertrude Stein: " 'I think writers *should* change their scenes; but . . . you would take nothing truly to the place where you went and so there would be nothing there until you had found it, and when you did find it, it would be something you had brought and thought you had left behind. And that would be creative recognition, too, because it would have all to do with you and nothing really to do with the place.' "

2. PB in taped conversation with LDS, in Santa Monica, California, 17–21 and 27 January 1969; hereafter abbreviated: Tape, LDS.

3. ALS, PB to Gertrude Stein, n.d.; in the Gertrude Stein Collection, the Beinecke Rare Book and Manuscript Library, Yale University Library. Material from this collection hereafter abbreviated: Yale.

4. TL, PB to Daniel Burns, n.d.; in the Paul Bowles Collection, Humanities Research Center, University of Texas at Austin. Material from this collection hereafter abbreviated: HRC.

5. Gertrude Stein, *Narration* (Chicago: University of Chicago Press, 1969), p. 29.

6. Gertrude Stein, *Wars I Have Seen* (New York: Random House, 1945), p. 23.

7. "If He Thinks: A Novelette of Desertion," *transition*, no. 10 (Jan. 1928), p. 9. A few years after she had met Bowles she modified her notion; cf. Gertrude Stein, *Everybody's Autobiography* (New York: Random House, 1937), p. 10: "I used to think the name of anybody was very important and the name made you and I have often said so. Perhaps I still think so but still there are so many names and anybody nowadays can call anybody any name they like."

8. Gertrude Stein, *Four in America* (New Haven: Yale University Press, 1947), pp. 3, 5. Even joining "Paul" to another name does not help much: "That makes it a little different although half of it is just the same" (p. 5).

9. PB in an interview with Ira Cohen, in Tangier in the early 1960s; hereafter abbreviated: Cohen interview. I am indebted to Mr. Cohen and to Andreas Brown for making available to me typescripts of that conversation.

10. Gertrude Stein, *Lectures in America* (1935; reprint ed., Boston: Beacon, 1957), pp. 233, 235, 236, 238.

11. Gertrude Stein, *Stanzas in Meditation* (New Haven: Yale University Press, 1956), pp. 208–9.

12. Alice Toklas in taped conversation with LDS, in Paris, 29 April 1960.

13. In his taped conversations with LDS, PB offered an additional motivation behind Gertrude Stein's directing him to Morocco: "She had just sent a few months earlier Kristians Tonny, one of her art protégés down there . . . and she wanted reports on him, and she thought she would use me for that, you see. And I became aware of that when I met Tonny and then he suggested that to me—he said he was sure that was why she sent me. And I wondered about that."

14. [Gertrude Stein], *The Autobiography of Alice B. Toklas* (New York: Harcourt, 1933), p. 309.

15. Gertrude Stein, "An American and France," in *What Are Masterpieces* (Los Angeles: Conference Press, 1940), pp. 62–64.

16. Oliver Evans, "An Interview with Paul Bowles," *Mediterranean Review* 1 (Winter 1971), 8; the interview (pp. 3–15) is hereafter abbreviated: Evans interview. The original interview took place in 1964 and was revised for this 1971 publication (TLS, PB to LDS, 29 April 1970).

17. Mark Twain, *The Innocents Abroad* (Hartford, Conn.: American, 1890), pp. 76, 88.

18. PB, "The Worlds of Tangier," *Holiday* 23 (March 1958), 66.

19. "The Years Move Outward (Scene I)," in TOS, p. 44.

20. TLS, PB to LDS, 15 Sept. 1960. For an early discussion of tea in Morocco—a ritual with pernicious effect on the nervous system (!) —cf. William Lempriere, *A Tour from Gibraltar to Tangier . . . [and] Morocco* (London, 1791), pp. 210–11, 298–300.

21. Thomas Mann, *Death in Venice,* trans. Kenneth Burke (New York: Knopf, 1929), p. 46.

22. *Paul Bowles in the Land of the Jumblies.* A film by Gary Conklin, 1969. The film was released in England in 1971 as *Paul Bowles in Morocco* and was shown in the United States on CBS's "Camera 3" in 1971 as *Paul Bowles' Morocco.*

23. *The Colossus of Maroussi* (1941; reprint ed., New York: New Directions, 1958), p. 190.

24. TLS, PB to LDS, 8 Sept. 1969. The 1958 story, "Sylvie Ann, the Boogie Man" in HAN, pp. 66-79, is based on other memories of the family laundress. Bowles now considers the story an inferior one and has excluded it from any American collection of his work.

25. Bowles asserted that the Chaamba "made life difficult for the French soldiers during the last part of the nineteenth century . . . ; now, like the rest of the Saharans, they are 'pacified,' but the legend of their cunning and ferocity still lives on in the market places and cafés of the towns, where tales are told" (Y, p. 9).

26. "Entity" and "identity" are, of course, Gertrude Stein's terms. She had always been one to encourage "entity," the writer's merging with his material—what Scott Fitzgerald called "living in story." The writer's emergence from his own creation, breaking the fusion of subject and object, profoundly troubled her aesthetic consciousness.

27. Harvey Breit, "Talk with Paul Bowles," *New York Times Book Review,* 9 March 1952, p. 19; hereafter abbreviated: Breit interview.

2 The Cold and Brilliant Morning

1. See WS, p. 274 for another version of this dream of Tangier. Alethea Hayter, *Opium and the Romantic Imagination* (Berkeley: University of Calif. Press, 1968), pp. 69-70 reminds us that "The gift of dreaming vividly in sleep was cherished and envied among the Romantic writers, as a necessary endowment of a poet." The "three cardinal

Romantic doctrines on dreams"—clearly fulfilled by Bowles in this experience—were "that they are a revelation of reality, that they can form and influence waking life, and that the dream process is a parallel and model of the process of poetic creation."

2. HRC owns the original typescript of "Pages from Cold Point," heavily emended in pencil and dated "July 1947 *M.S.* '*Ferncape.*' " Presumably it was from this ms. that PB made a final copy for *Wake*. The missing copy text reduced the original manuscript, eliminating the opening three and the penultimate paragraphs and making a new penultimate paragraph of two sentences salvaged from the discarded opening. (The original typescript had also contained a half-page double-spaced political discussion between Norton and Racky, which did not appear, evidently, in the copy text.) *Wake*, following the typescript, used asterisks to separate journal entries.

The same year of the *Wake* publication, the anthology *New Directions in Prose and Poetry. Number 11* (New York: New Directions, 1949), pp. 202–23, included the story and gave copyright credit to *Wake*. The *New Directions* text is *not*, however, *Wake*'s. Instead, it is close to the corrected original typescript preserved at HRC. How it got into print remains unclear; but that version seems not to have been republished. In 1950 the *Wake* text was adopted for *The Delicate Prey and Other Stories*. Subsequent anthologists have drawn it from that volume and thereby introduced another error: *The Delicate Prey* text omitted the asterisks and used wide spacing to distinguish separate journal entries. "Much later, but I feel no better . . ." (DP, p. 189) thus begins a page; but the remark is not a continuation of that entry which concluded the preceding page. The book's typography does not make this clear, and anthologists therefore incorrectly combine the two entries.

Cyril Connolly wrote PB 27 Sept. 1949 that he would like the story (which he called "Trouble at Cold Point") for *Horizon:* "I would like to try to overcome the printer's scruples once again" (HRC). He failed (Maugham advised him not even to try [TLS, PB to LDS, 8 Sept. 1969]), and

"Pages from Cold Point" was not published in Britain until 1968; then it came out first in *Nova* magazine and second in a new collection of Bowles's short stories, *Pages from Cold Point and Other Stories* (London: Peter Owen, 1966), pp. 7–35. He gave the collection that title to celebrate the story's publication there after twenty years. Both British publications altered *The Delicate Prey* text, particularly in vocabulary and punctuation. Neither British text has authorial approval.

3. *Advertisements for Myself* (New York: Putnam's, 1959), p. 468.

4. Cf. rough draft of letter, PB to "Irving," ca. 1957 (HRC): "What is an intellectual? . . . I know what *I* mean by the word: a man whose personal scales of value are so weighted that concepts are always heavier than anything else. . . . we are obliged to transform our impulses into fairly precise concepts before we can deal with them, a necessity which carries with it advantages as well as the opposite. . . . I can't subscribe to your conviction that you have the 'right' to a pleasant life merely because you can conceive of such a thing and so far consider you have been more than normally deprived of it. God knows I think everyone has to try to find such a thing, but I *know* it is false to think that one 'deserves' anything at all. Thinking that is equivalent to making the statement which is the ultimate in absurdity: 'Life is (good) (bad) (inexplicable) (simple) (any other adjective). What quality can existence possibly have? How can one merit anything?"

5. WS, p. 100: "Although I knew enough Freud to believe that the sex urge was an important mainspring of life, it still seemed to me that any conscious manifestation of sex was necessarily ludicrous. Defecation and copulation were two activities which made a human being totally ridiculous." In *The Sheltering Sky*, Bowles was to make much of the associations among ingestion, digestion, and defecation. Port's death scene is filled with images of blood and excrement, almost an obsessive connection for Bowles. On p. 57, for example, he had ended a paragraph with Port drinking alone in the bar. Bowles then added a line to the typescript: "Somewhere in the hotel a toilet was flushed,

making its sounds of choking and regurgitation." The reference to the cloaca becomes central in this imagery (SS, p. 214).

6. HRC has an untitled TS which may have been the opening for an uncompleted story but seems pertinent to this discussion: "I want to make it clear at the outset that I have a completely hands off attitude when it comes to judging the morality of other people's behavior. . . . I can never be sure which I ought to do, so that being caught in that indecision I end up feeling absolutely nothing one way or the other. And if you don't feel that a thing is either good or bad, how can you express yourself on it? The best thing is to keep quiet about it. I've been told that this characteristic indicates either profound selfishness or great lack of imagination. It could be both. I don't think it's of any importance. In fact, I don't think anyone should ever take other people's criticism of his character seriously. It will just cause confusion inside." Cf. SH, p. 343: "A little sentence he [Stenham] had once read came into his head: *Happy is the man who believes he is happy.* Yes, he thought, and more accursed than the murderer is the man who works to destroy that belief."

7. Norton and Racky were based on a father and his adopted son whom Bowles had known in Cuernavaca, Los Angeles, and New York (Tape, LDS). The setting itself was probably influenced by Bowles's stay at Ocho Rios, when he was translating Giraudoux's *La Folle de Chaillot* (cf. WS, p. 272).

8. An undated notebook entry (HRC) begins: "One of the great problems with which a man in my circumstances has to deal is the problem of boredom. Once you have felt a twinge of it there is no hope of shaking it off—at least, not here in a place like this—and although you can invent a thousand ways of forgetting it or of making its presence less unpleasant,—(best thing to accept and study it,)—a kind of repulsion of the spirit against meeting its image, against entering into mirror as it were." PB says (TLS to LDS, 6 Jan. 1973) that this was intended to be made eventually into a journal entry by Norton.

9. Quoted in Enid Starkie, *Flaubert: The Making of the*

Master (New York: Atheneum, 1967), p. 339. For an interesting discussion of the same passage, cf. Robert Martin Adams, *Nil: Episodes in the Literary Conquest of Void during the Nineteenth Century* (London and New York: Oxford, 1966), pp. 68–69. Adams also discusses the concept of Nothing in Poe, a writer whose poems and tales influenced Bowles. Cf. Bowles's dedication of *The Delicate Prey*: *"for my mother, who first read me the stories of Poe."*

10. TLS, PB to LDS, 8 Sept. 1969: "Oran is the city of the opening and closing of SKY. No use trying to identify the other towns. I carefully jumbled them as I wrote. I suppose Sbâ is really Béni Abbès, and certainly Bou Noura is Ghardaïa. Ain Krorfa is Laghouat, El Gâa is El Goléa, and so on. No importance." Actual towns mentioned in the book are Tessalit and Adrar.

11. *Wars I Have Seen* (New York: Random House, 1945), p. 258; similar ideas appeared earlier in *Everybody's Autobiography* (New York: Random House, 1937), pp. 198, 202–3. Gertrude Stein had complained that in America "there is no sky, there is no lid on top of them and so they move around or stand still and do not say anything" (pp. 202–3).

12. C. G. Jung, *Memories, Dreams, Reflections,* ed. Aniela Jaffé, trans. Richard and Clara Winston (New York: Vintage, 1963), pp. 240–41, 242.

13. Eugène Delacroix, *Selected Letters, 1813–1863,* trans. Jean Stewart (New York: St. Martin's, 1971), p. 186.

14. André Gide, *Pretexts,* ed. Justin O'Brien, trans. Jeffrey J. Carre (London: Secker & Warburg, 1959), p. 144.

15. "I don't feel that I am [an existentialist]. I certainly don't follow along with Sartre about the necessity for choice and all that sort of thing. But what is an existentialist character, really? It's one who plays it by ear and every moment afresh from the given situation. He's infinitely adaptable, I would say. He thinks of everything in terms of the immediate situation—not according to credos and tradition." Bowles's own attitudes somewhat parallel but do not merge with existential notions: "The destruction of the ego has always seemed an important thing. I took it for granted

that that was what really one was looking for in order to attain knowledge and the ability to live, to know that one's living life to the best of one's ability. . . . It's the stripping away of all the things that differentiate one person from another person. By stripping them away one arrives at a sort of basic working truth which will help one to go on. What's important, in other words, is not the ways in which you're different from other people but the way in which you're conscious of being like other people" (Tape, LDS).

16. Rough draft of letter, PB to "Jay" Laughlin, n.d.: "I have been thinking about the 'harem' business for publicity. Do you think by any chance it would be giving the story away? In the blurb of the Lehmann catalogue [Lehmann had already published the novel in England] various sexual possibilities were hinted at without mentioning the actual material of the climax (if the flight across the desert, the love-making with the two Arabs at once, the wedding and the escape can be called a climax!)" (HRC).

17. Copy inscribed to John Stuart Groves (HRC). The novel's innkeeper, Abdelkader, had the same name as an Arab (*not* an innkeeper) Bowles had known; see WS, p. 134. Originally Bowles had called Kit "Kate"; by the time he had come to chapter 3, he had settled upon Kit. Tunner, on the other hand, had been Turner throughout the first typescript; the name was corrected by holograph only after that typescript had been completed. (George Turner was an American PB met in Ghardaïa in 1933. See WS, pp. 158–62.) PB concedes that there is a more than nominal similarity between Port and Paul.

18. HRC owns three drafts of the novel. The earliest seems to have begun as a fair copy of an earlier (non-existent) draft of the first two chapters. (Presumably in them Kit had been called Kate.) The typescript used asterisks to break up sections; it was then cut up into chapters and the fragments pasted down on sheets of conforming size. Page numbers were assigned only after the typescript was thus glued down and assembled; they number 253. The typescript has holograph corrections throughout. HRC has a carbon of that typescript, but not cut up and paginated

accurately. (Not all of the breaks asterisked were converted into chapters.) The carbon importantly reveals revisions PB made in the typewriter (since careful erasures in the original typescript concealed several of them). HRC's third type-script is a carbon of a presumed-lost final typescript (sent to a publisher?). This typescript also has revisions and is not identical with the published text. Either another typescript followed it (which is unlikely) or else further changes were made in the galleys and/or page proofs. (The physical de-scriptions of the three principals, for instance [SS, pp. 13–15], appear in none of these typescripts.) The English edition, published by John Lehmann in September 1949, has British usages not in the American edition, published by New Directions in December 1949. The English edition also has some lines omitted from the American text. PB's recol-lection is: "I sent out two separate scripts—one to Con-necticut, and one to London. Lehmann was three months quicker in getting it out. Perhaps I made the changes my-self when I retyped it. In both instances I corrected proofs, but each set was corrected using its own manuscript. Who knows what happened?" (TLS, PB to LDS, 8 Jan. 1972). Signet Books reset the New Directions text and, in Janu-ary 1951, issued the novel as a paperback. Bowles remem-bers: "I worked over a separate ms. for Victor Weybright there at New American Editions" (TLS, PB to LDS, 20 Feb. 1973). The Signet edition set the opening chapter in italics and added an epigraph to the dedication page: " 'G igherdh ish'ed our illi' 'No man is master of his fate'— Berber song." (But the phrase itself, untranslated, had already appeared twice in chapter 27 of both the Lehmann and New Directions editions.) The Signet edition was re-printed in Dec. 1955, but those revisions were not incor-porated by New Directions in its own later printings.

19. "Almost All the Apples Are Gone," an abandoned novel which PB had begun in the summer of 1949, de-veloped these themes. It was to have been the first-person narrative by a New England schoolteacher who quits aca-demic life and goes off to Central America. There, she marries a plantation owner and eventually has an affair

with a native, a gardener on the estate. She becomes pregnant by him, but the husband (ignorant of the affair) dies before the birth of the child. When the gardener tries to take over the plantation, she has him imprisoned on trumped-up murder charges. As the estate decays she turns to fortune-telling, predicting for the dark native women the good fortune of a light-skinned child. She also supplies them with her vain and stupid son, whose impregnation of them fulfills her prophecy. When the son eventually abandons his mother and the plantation for a job in town, she replaces him with a white half-wit. The gardener is released from prison and returns. Thinking the half-wit is his son grown up, he again tries to take control of the property, and this time the mother incites the "son" to kill him. Bowles gave up the novel before it had progressed very far, but he did not forget the sexual relationship that supported it. In the early 1960s, when he began *Up Above the World*, he redeveloped some of these themes in the half-breed Grove and his Canadian mother, Mrs. Rainmantle—whom Grove arranges to have murdered. (Further complicating these generational difficulties: in an early version of *Up Above the World*, Mrs. Rainmantle is a lesbian who bridges the generations by assigning her affections to a beautiful young American girl who herself is enduring marriage to a much older, retired doctor.) For a discussion of *Up Above the World*, see my "*Up Above the World* So High," in *The Mystery & Detection Annual* (Beverly Hills, Calif.: Donald Adams, 1973).

20. I had once been told that Peggy Glanville-Hicks had been the model for Mrs. Lyle and asked PB for confirmation. TLS, PB to LDS, 2 June 1972: "There's absolutely no connection between them. Mrs. Lyle is taken from a . . . [woman] whom I kept running into wherever I went in 1947; she had her son with her. Most of the scenes between Mrs. Lyle and her son Eric were more or less literal accounts of the scenes I witnessed in Fez, Tangier, Algeciras, Ronda and Cordoba between August and November. Peggy Glanville-Hicks, indeed!" Also cf. TLS, PB to LDS, 26 Nov. 1972: "I have no idea as to whether there *was* incest; I

should think it extremely unlikely. But they did always share a room, and he did say to me: Isn't married life wonderful? Nada mas."

21. SS, p. 163. Mohammed, the hotelkeeper, had caught the Lyles in bed together and, in the original typescript, accuses Eric: "You have been making love with her" (SS, p. 143). The emphasis upon the undoubted sexual relationship between the Lyles contrasts sadly with the doubtful sexual relationship between the Moresbys.

22. SS, p. 16: originally, when listening to the aria on the radio in Oran, Port complains: "Every piece of that sort of music is like a model life; you know long before just when it's going to die, and just what kind of death it's going to have." By "model" he means: "Model life, model town, model country. The worst possible." Similarly, pp. 74–75, analyzing Port's dream, originally went into detail on the associational processes of Port's mind.

23. His account of how he wrote his story, "You Are Not I" (published in England as "A Spring Day"), is illustrative: "I remember one night I woke up having—funny, I didn't see it as clearly, the story, in my dream, as I saw the words I was writing. The words were imposed on the scenes, as it could be on the screen, you know. But I was writing the text on top of the scenes . . . just enough for me to get into it. The whole atmosphere of the beginning I had dreamed. So when I woke up I began writing, without putting the light on, in the dark—I could barely read it the next day. I just wrote, large, and turned pages and kept this up, because I was saying it from memory, almost. Down as far as putting the stones in the mouths, and then there was no more and I just went on, because I had for me what I thought was a good beginning the next day" (Tape, LDS).

24. Two years after *The Sheltering Sky* was published, Bowles again discussed *le baptême de la solitude:* "It is a unique sensation, and it has nothing to do with loneliness, for loneliness presupposes memory. Here, in this wholly mineral landscape lighted by stars like flares, even memory disappears; nothing is left but your own breathing and the sound of your heart beating. A strange, and by no means

pleasant, process of reintegration begins inside you. . . . For no one who has stayed in the Sahara for a while is quite the same as when he came" (HAG, p. 143). HRC typescript dated "Tangier 1951."

25. *The Koran,* trans. N. J. Dawood (London: Penguin, 1956), p. 60.

26. Hayter, *Opium and the Romantic Imagination,* p. 157; see also p. 152 for remarks about the contribution of opium to Baudelaire's visionary experience: "prepared hashish contains a small amount of opium as well as its main constituents of *Cannabis indica* and butter." But Bowles states that "there is no opium in majoun here in Morocco" (TLS, PB to LDS, 16 Feb. 1973).

27. Jane Bowles, *Collected Works* (New York: Farrar, 1966), p. 392.

28. PB, "The Secret Sahara," *Holiday* 13 (Jan. 1953), 88. HRC typescript is dated 1951. HAG, pp. 157–58 reprints this with modifications.

3 The Hours after Noon

1. Bowles had wanted the collection labeled *The Delicate Prey*—perhaps to emphasize the applicability of that title to all of these tales. His agent persuaded him that such a title, unqualified by "And Other Stories," suggests a novel; sales would be adversely affected by the return of books bought under a misapprehension. (HRC: TLS, Helen Strauss to PB, 12 Oct. 1950).

2. "How Many Midnights," "A Thousand Days for Mokhtar," "Tea on the Mountain," "Pages from Cold Point," and "The Delicate Prey." The first three were given British publication in *The Hours after Noon;* the last two, in *Pages from Cold Point.*

3. Edmondo de Amicis, *Morocco: Its People and Places,* trans. Maria Hornor Lansdale (Philadelphia: Coates, 1897), 2: 35. PB told LDS he was well acquainted with this two-volume work. The Filala were masters at torture. Mulai Abdallah "originated the horrible punishment of sewing a

living man into the disemboweled body of a bull that they might rot together" (Ibid., p. 36). In *The Spider's House* (p. 120), Si Driss reminds his son Amar that the Alaoui dynasty "let the carrion French into Morocco," and he quotes the old saying: "The reign of the Filala: it's not costly but it's not cheap. It's not noisy but it's not quiet. You have a king but you have no king. That's the reign of the Filala."

4. *Staying on Alone: Letters of Alice B. Toklas*, ed. Edward Burns (New York: Liveright, 1973), p. 220 prints the full text of the 9 January letter; pp. 188–89 print a portion of the 22 February 1950 letter. For more about the interest that Alice Toklas and Gertrude Stein took in mystery and detective fiction, see my "Gertrude Stein and the Vital Dead," in *The Mystery & Detection Annual* (Beverly Hills, Calif.: Donald Adams, 1972), pp. 102–23.

5. "The Hours after Noon" first appeared in *Zero Anthology, No. 8*, ed. Themistocles Hoetis (New York: Zero, 1956), pp. 197–236. Earlier attempts to publish it had failed. On 12 Oct. 1950 Helen Strauss wrote PB that the story had been rejected by *Mademoiselle, Harpers Bazaar, Atlantic, Flair, Harper's, Tomorrow, Holiday, Partisan Review, Sewanee Review,* and *Cosmopolitan:* "it's now with Yale Review." In 1959, the story (revised in some slight details) appeared in, and titled, Bowles's second British collection of short stories and in 1967 was reprinted in *The Time of Friendship.*

6. So in corrected typescript; all printings eliminate the "non." Confirming the correctness of the typescript is a line in the next paragraph of the printed text: "Vaguely she knew that his [a Moroccan's] arrival would entail something unpleasant, but for the moment she refused to think about it."

7. *Gertrude Stein on Picasso*, ed. Edward Burns (New York: Liveright, 1970), p. 65.

8. In the summer of 1949 Bowles began a novel, "Almost All the Apples Are Gone," and had written several pages of it in a pink notebook that he was carrying with him to Ceylon that December. When the sight of Tangier suddenly

made him want to write about Morocco instead of New York and Central America, the scenes of his projected work, he took this same notebook and began writing in it, starting on the final page and working from back to front. When he reached what was approximately published page 192 he stopped: he had filled the notebook and run smack into the "Apples" MS. What manuscript Bowles then wrote to complete his novel seems not to have been saved. The MS history of *Let It Come Down* thus devolves upon this one pink notebook, whose back cover as well as several contiguous pages are missing, but which does contain 176 manuscript pages relating to *Let It Come Down*. The extant bound –MS starts "strides, threw himself full length on the crackling leaves . . ." (LICD, p. 92) and presents all of chapter 8, as well as notes for chapter 9 before it begins with chapter 1. Besides giving the earliest draft for the first 192 pages of the novel (as well as some incidental episodes used in later sections of the novel), this notebook has graphs, charts, notations, and commentary on the ensuing events and confirms all of Bowles's statements about how he worked on the book.

9. A notebook entry may illuminate the problem, as well as the author's attitude: "At the Beidaoui party [chap. 10], writer & wife [Mr. and Mrs. Richard Holland]. (The intellectual) Someone says: 'When you're writing a book, don't you have to think of it as the greatest thing ever done?' 'Good God, no! I've never thought of anything I wrote, at any time, as anything but uninspired tripe.' 'But then how can you create?' 'I do it, and that's enough. If an artist is the kind of man who needs to think his work is good, he'll generally find a way to think it. Unfort. most do.' (Episode of starved kittens in alley.) (Writer's remarks about disappear of atmosphere from air.)" (HRC). The episode of the starved kittens concludes the party and chapter 12 in the published novel.

10. "One is convinced that it is good to be in No Country, to feel, in this world of swiftly increasing social organization and hypertrophied governments, that anarchy is still a possibility. . . . It is a pleasant thing to be in a place

where one can at least have the illusion that the individual still has charge" ("Letter from Tangier," *London Magazine* 1 [July 1954], 51). The theory of life as anarchy occurred to Dyar as he lay on the beach: "life is not a movement toward or away from anything; not even from the past to the future, or from youth to old age, or from birth to death. The whole of life does not equal the sum of its parts. It equals any one of the parts; there is no sum" (LICD, p. 186).

11. "Letter from Tangier," pp. 51–52.

12. "The word *m'hashish* (equivalent in Moghrebi of 'behashished' or 'full of hashish') is used not only in a literal sense, but also figuratively, to describe a person whose behaviour seems irrational or unexpected" (Paul Bowles's jacket blurb for Mohammed Mrabet's *M'Hashish*, translated by Paul Bowles [San Francisco: City Lights, 1969]).

13. HRC: Untitled 15 pp. PB TS on Fez, written in 1960 for *Life International*. Presumably unpublished.

14. *London Magazine* 1 (June 1954), 84–88.

15. HRC has a catalog for an art show by Ahmed Yacoubi at New York City's Amici Gallery, ca. 1965. It quotes a 1957 statement by PB: "Ahmed Yacoubi was born in 1931 in El Keddane, one of the most ancient quarters of Fez. He is a Cherif on both his father's and mother's side; that is to say, his parents are both direct descendants of the Prophet Mohammed. His paternal grandfather and his father exercised the profession of f'qih, which means that they healed by the laying on of hands, by the manipulation of fire, by collecting herbs and brewing concoctions of them, and, most important, by the writing of sacred formulas at propitious moments. The office of f'qih was destined to be assumed by Ahmed; his education consisted solely of learning how to treat the sick, of learning the legends, songs and dances of his region, and of memorizing and paraphrasing the Koran." For further evidence of Yacoubi's culinary power that is "based on the traditions of Moroccan alchemy," see Ahmed Yacoubi, *Alchemist's Cookbook*, ed. Sherry Needham (Tucson, Arizona: Omen, 1972).

16. Two 1953–54 articles draw heavily upon the friendship with Yacoubi: "A Man Must Not Be Very Moslem,"

HAG, pp. 74–96 is a revision of "Europe's Most Exotic City," *Holiday* 17 (May 1955). (Each version contains considerable material not printed in the other. HAG dates these journal entries 25 Sept.–19 Oct. 1953.) The 1954 article, "Mustapha and His Friends," HAG, pp. 59–73, is a revision of "The Incredible Arab," *Holiday* 20 (August 1956). HAG omits the anecdote of a woman who turned a man into a donkey, though it was later told by PB in the film, *Paul Bowles in the Land of the Jumblies.*

17. Rom Landau, *Moroccan Drama, 1900–1955* (London: Robert Hale, 1956), p. 315. This book surveys the political events antecedent to *The Spider's House,* and I have drawn the cited historical facts from it.

18. HRC has two notebooks of manuscript for *The Spider's House.* A brown notebook, whose first 68 pages have been torn away, starts (MS p. 69) with Book One. In general this holograph (MS pp. 69–257) is close to the published version; the journal omits the story of Amar's life as a potter, but otherwise gives the experience as published, pp. 15–30, 67–135, 267–318, and 321–27. A mottled green notebook, the first section of which is Bowles's journal for Ceylon and South India, contains additional material: the published pages 318–21, 328–44, and 353–406. The published chapter 29 does not appear in these journals; also missing is the prologue. Chapter 29 was supplied later by Bowles, at the insistence of Bennett Cerf and Donald Klopfer, who "felt that there should be a specific love scene between the man [Stenham] and the woman [Polly], as though it were a Hollywood film, because that's the way they publish. I was indignant and annoyed, naturally, by the suggestion, and I held out—but not successfully—and then I wrote it, but my own way, and it wasn't *that* bad, you know. It didn't really violate the book, but it wasn't what I wanted" (Tape, LDS). The prologue may also have been a late addition, a melodramatic attempt to begin *in medias res* and to give what is otherwise a sensibly presented serious novel the shock appeal of an exotic mystery. Needless to say, that prologue sets a false tone for the novel which follows.

19. "*Baraka* might be called white magic. It is simply the

power to work beneficently, and can be accomplished in any manner. The amulets worn by the Moroccans to ward off evil are called barakas. And a man can have baraka, although almost a certain provision is that he be a Cherif" (TLS, PB to LDS, 1 August 1973).

4 The Twilight Hour of the Storyteller

1. Bowles speaks French, Spanish, and Moghrebi, and reads Italian. His first translations were done in the early 1930s from the French and the Italian for *Modern Music*. As a member of the editorial board for *View* in the 1940s he did "most of their translations: poems, articles, stories, bits of novels—French and Spanish" (Tape, LDS). In the spring of 1945 he translated Sartre's *Huis Clos as No Exit*; and twice he has translated Garcia-Lorca to create a libretto for his own operas, *The Wind Remains* and *Yerma*. In 1952 Prentice-Hall published his translation of Frison-Roche's novel, *La Piste Oubliée*, as *The Lost Trail of the Sahara*.

2. "If there's a word or a phrase that seems to have any kind of equivocal meaning or ramifications of meaning, I stop the machine—I never do it alone, never do it without the author there—and we get to the bottom of it, that's all, just for my benefit. Then if it seems that it's not clear to the average reader—it's got to be clear to people who have never been to Morocco, obviously—then I say 'You're going to have to record a few more sentences, explaining this.' Which he will generally do, though sometimes he doesn't want to, whoever he is" (Tape, LDS).

3. Mohammed Mrabet, "Talking to Daniel Halpern," *Transatlantic Review* 39 (Spring 1971), 126. "As Mr. Mrabet prefers to speak in Spanish when talking to non-Moslems, the interview was conducted in Spanish and afterwards translated into English by Mr. Bowles." Jane Bowles always spoke to both Larbi Layachi and Mrabet in Moghrebi; the custom seems to be that whatever language a person first uses with a Moroccan, that language he always uses with that Moroccan.

4. Richard Rumbold's "An Evening with Paul Bowles," *London Magazine* 7 (November 1960), 65–73, purportedly an account of hashish experimentation supervised by Bowles, "is pretty subjective, not accurate" (TLS, PB to LDS, 8 Sept. 1969). Rumbold first met Bowles in December 1954 when they were fellow passengers, bound for Ceylon. Rumbold's diary, *A Message in Code,* ed. William Plomer (London: Weidenfeld and Nicolson, 1964), has numerous references to Bowles and reveals "a kind of adolescent yearning towards him, to be like him or something. I love him dearly" (p. 285). They lived near each other in Ceylon for some months in 1955 and then saw each other again in Morocco in 1960. The reported evening was 19 February 1960; but Rumbold's diary proves that in his article he incorporated many other, nonhashish, experiences he had had with Bowles five years earlier. And some of Bowles's remarks, here attributed to or analytical of hashish, had in their original context nothing at all to do with it. The journal entries about the hashish experience itself seem, however, authentic: "The effect of hashish," wrote Rumbold, "is not to give pleasure, except incidentally . . . but rather to pass one's emotions in review, giving them a concrete 'feel' and enabling one to regard them with a certain detachment; and this, not unlike analysis, has a liberating effect. . . . [Bowles] claims to have derived much benefit from hashish and he is certainly extremely clear-headed and intelligent. . . . [Bowles] remarked that hashish taught him the value and enjoyment of the present moment. Under hashish one's problems seems to focus, one concentrates on them as on a novel. . . . Hashish de-intensifies life, and consequently should leave one calmer. Hashish is a lonely, isolating experience, in which each man grapples with his problems. . . . [Bowles] says one must be experienced to do it alone" (p. 284).

5. PB, "Kif—Prologue and Compendium of Terms," in *The Book of Grass,* ed. George Andrews and Simon Vinkenoog (New York: Grove, 1967), p. 111. He has said of his own work: "The character *as character* is not important. The character is acting out a situational drama in a given setting, and the whole thing is one thing—that is, the character, the setting, the mood, the action, the situation. The

character's not apart from his situation (in that sense it's existentialist—I suppose that's what they mean). The character does not exist in my writing apart from where he is and in what situation he is and what is happening to him. He is not a person outside of that. It's a closed circuit" (Tape, LDS).

6. Richard Rumbold's diary also testifies to Boujemaa's appeal. On 20 March 1960, a month after his "hashish evening" with Bowles in Tangier, Rumbold was in Marra-kech: "In the evening Paul met a young Arab friend, Boujemaa, and we drank mint tea with him." The next day Boujemaa took Rumbold and his aunt through the souks—leading Rumbold to conclude that "Marrakesh has far more charm than Tangier." On 29 March, Rumbold, his aunt, and Bowles left, with Boujemaa, for Tangier, via Mogador and Rabat. Rumbold flew back to England in mid-April but returned to Tangier late in July and resumed his relationship with He of the Assembly. On 8 August, Rumbold noted: "I doubt whether there exists a more affectionate, decent and forthcoming companion than Bou-jemaa." Their moments together had made Rumbold "calm and in high spirits." In September, Rumbold left Morocco permanently. On 5 March 1961 he wrote Bowles: "I have thought so often of our friendship, of your original mind and sensibility, of your great kindness of heart, and of all the fun we had together about this time last year." He added that he would like to keep in touch with Boujemaa "because I think he is a loyal and good soul." Eight days later, in Palermo, Rumbold fell from his hotel window and was killed instantly.

7. Bowles recorded the aphorism in his notebook: " 'A pipe of kif in the morning before breakfast gives a man the strength of a hundred camels in the patio.' " (HRC). The title page of A Hundred Camels in the Courtyard called this epigraph a "Nchaioui Proverb."

8. The soupkettle fantasy "came from Ahmed Yacoubi, a story that he himself made up one night ten years before I actually wrote 'He of the Assembly,' which remained in my mind. He was very high on majoun" (Tape, LDS).

9. HRC has several versions of this novella. The holograph MS is in two separate notebooks; other notebooks contain sentences, fragments of paragraphs, and suggestions for plot development. The 58-page original typescript was untitled, though the working title for the holograph material had been "Fräulein Windling"; this typescript has numerous holograph emendations. (The published title, "The Time of Friendship," was scrawled at the top of the first page of this typescript, probably when the manuscript was sold to Andreas Brown.) "Master copy, original version (discarded)" is the second typescript (47 pp.); it is titled "The War of the Wise Men." A third original typescript (44 pp.) is titled "*The War of the Wise Men.*" The carbon of this third typescript is marked "(Original version), 1961. Carbon." Only on it has "A Time of Friendship" been written in as title, replacing the heavily canceled "The War of the Wise Men."

10. PB, "The Moslems," *Holiday* 25 (April 1959), 108. HAG, p. 39 prints a portion of only the concluding sentence. HRC typescript is dated "Tangier 1955."

11. Originally Fräulein Windling was to have been less meditative and more analytical: "Moonless nights were quieter, but the sound of the dogs, yapping and yelping, to each other in the dark from one garden to another, was always there somewhere this side of silence. Fräulein Windling was pleased to have discovered a pattern in the dogs' communication. She had made a graph based on three weeks of clocking the phenomenon, and discovered that there were smaller variations within the lunar curve" (HRC).

Selected Bibliography

In the first section are Bowles's main works and translations, listed chronologically. In the second section are some fugitive works which were not referred to in the notes to my book but which nonetheless relate to some of its concerns.

Main Works

Sartre, Jean-Paul. *No Exit*. Translated by Paul Bowles. New York: Samuel French, 1946.

The Sheltering Sky. London: John Lehmann, 1949; New York: New Directions, 1949.

A Little Stone: Stories. London: John Lehmann, 1950.

The Delicate Prey and Other Stories. New York: Random House, 1950. Reprint. New York: Ecco, 1972. Contains contents of *A Little Stone*, plus five other stories.

Let It Come Down. New York: Random House, 1952; London: John Lehmann, 1952.

Frison-Roche, Roger. *The Lost Trail of the Sahara*. Translated by Paul Bowles. New York: Prentice-Hall, 1952.

The Spider's House. New York: Random House, 1955; London: Macdonald, 1957.

Yallah. Text by Paul Bowles; photographs by Peter W. Haeberlin. New York: McDowell, Obolensky, 1957; London: Merlin, 1957.

The Hours after Noon: Short Stories. London: Heinemann, 1959.

A Hundred Camels in the Courtyard. San Francisco: City Lights, 1962.

Their Heads Are Green and Their Hands Are Blue. New York: Random House, 1963.

Their Heads Are Green. London: Peter Owen, 1963.

Layachi, Larbi [Driss ben Hamed Charhadi]. *A Life Full of Holes.* "A Novel Tape-recorded in Moghrebi and Translated into English by Paul Bowles." New York: Grove, 1964; London: Weidenfeld & Nicolson, 1964.

Up Above the World: A Novel. New York: Simon & Schuster, 1966; London: Peter Owen, 1967.

The Time of Friendship: A Volume of Short Stories. New York: Rinehart and Winston, 1967.

Mrabet, Mohammed. *Love with a Few Hairs.* "Taped and Translated from the Moghrebi by Paul Bowles." London: Peter Owen, 1967; New York: Braziller, 1968.

Pages from Cold Point and Other Stories. London: Peter Owen, 1968.

Scenes [poems]. Los Angeles: Black Sparrow, 1968.

Mrabet, Mohammed. *M'Hashish* [stories]. "Taped and translated from the Moghrebi by Paul Bowles." San Francisco: City Lights, 1969.

————. *The Lemon.* "Translated from the Moghrebi and edited by Paul Bowles in collaboration with Mohammed Mrabet." London: Peter Owen, 1969; New York: McGraw-Hill, 1972.

The Thicket of Spring: Poems 1926–1969. Los Angeles: Black Sparrow, 1972.

Without Stopping: An Autobiography. New York: Putnam's, 1972; London: Peter Owen, 1972.

Bowles, Paul and Mohammed Mrabet. *The Boy Who Set the Fire & Other Stories.* "Taped & translated from the Moghrebi by Paul Bowles." Los Angeles: Black Sparrow, 1974.

Choukri, Mohamed. *For Bread Alone.* Translated by Paul Bowles. London: Peter Owen, forthcoming.

————. *Jean Genet in Tangier.* Translated by Paul Bowles. New York: Ecco, forthcoming.

Fugitive Works

"Bluey." By "Paul Bowles—aged 9." *View* 3 (October 1943), 81–82. Reprinted in *A Night with Jupiter and Other*

Fantastic Stories. Edited by Charles Henri Ford. New York: View, 1945.

Scenes from the Door [two songs]. Music by Paul Bowles; words by Gertrude Stein. Fez, Morocco; Éditions de la Vipère, 1934.

"Letter to Freddy" [song]. *New Music*, April 1935, pp. 12–14. Music by Paul Bowles; words by Gertrude Stein.

Visconti, Luchino. *Two Screenplays: La Terra Trema; Senso*. Translated by Judith Green. New York: Orion, 1970. Tennessee Williams and Paul Bowles were, on the screen, given dialogue credit for *Senso* (which, in the United States was released as *Wanton Countess*). This publication omits such credit.

"Majoun Keddane" [recipe]. In *The Artists' & Writers' Cookbook*. Foreword by Alice B. Toklas. Edited by Beryl Barr and Barbara Turner Sachs. Sausalito, Calif.: Contact, 1961. Bowles's recipe "comes from Fez and has nothing to do with the one Alice Toklas included in her book which was from El Ksar El Kebir."

Boulaich, Abdeslam. "Three Hekayas." Taped and translated from the Moghrebi by Paul Bowles. *Genesis West* 1 (September 1962), 3–7. Reprinted in *Antaeus*, no. 2 (Spring 1971), 125–29.

"Afternoon with Antaeus" [story]. *Antaeus*, no. 1 (Summer 1970), 7–10. Bowles is Consulting Editor for this publication and to it contributes translations as well as original prose and poetry.

"On Isabelle Eberhardt." *Antaeus*, no. 6 (Summer 1972), 77–78. See Bowles's translation from the French of Eberhardt's "Criminal," pp. 79–83, and "The Oblivion Seekers," pp. 84–85.

Choukri, Mohamed. "For Bread Alone." Translated from the Arabic by Paul Bowles and Mohamed Choukri. *Antaeus*, no. 7 (Autumn 1972), 85–96.

Herbert, David. *Second Son: An Autobiography*. Foreword by Paul Bowles. London: Peter Owen, 1972.

"Etiquette" [poem]. In *The Mystery & Detection Annual*. Beverly Hills, Calif.: Donald Adams, 1972.

Index

Adrar, Algeria, 49, 152n10
Aid el Kebir (Moslem festival), 101–2, 103
Algeciras, Spain, 58, 155n20
Algeria. *See* Oran, Algeria; *The Sheltering Sky*; "The Time of Friendship"
"Almost All the Apples Are Gone" (Bowles's abandoned novel), 154n19, 158n8
Alteration of consciousness by drugs and magic: Bowles's attitude to magic, 28, 111, 119–20, 125–26, 127–28, 161n19; Bowles eats majoun, 66–67, 68, 113, 114, 115; hashish, 67; Bowles tries marijuana, 67, 114; hashish in Bowles's fiction, 78–79, 95, 113, 117–18, 160n12; majoun in Bowles's fiction, 92; kif in Bowles's fiction, 95, 97, 117–18, 124, 126, 127; Bowles smokes kif, 113, 114, 115–16, 125; Bowles tries ether, 114; Bowles tries hypnosis, 114; Bowles's attitude toward alcohol, 114, 118–19; "kif story" defined, 117, 118–19, 128; djaoui, 123–24,

125–26; relationship of majoun to opium, 157n26; Bowles's hashish evening with Rumbold, 163n4
Amicis, Edmondo de. *See* De Amicis, Edmondo
Apollinaire, Guillaume, 131

Barbary. *See* Morocco
Barber, Samuel, 37
Baudelaire, Charles: quoted by Bowles, 81, 91; mentioned, 67, 98, 114, 157n26
Béni Abbès, Algeria, 49, 152n10
Big Table (magazine), 129
Biskra, Algeria, 18
Boujemaa. *See* "He of the Assembly"
Boulanger, Nadia, 4, 16
Bou-Saada, Algeria, 18
Bowles, Jane: "Camp Cataract," 69; an enemy of cannabis, 116–17; mentioned, 162n3
Bowles, Paul: early years, 2–4; at University of Virginia, 2–4; interested in painting, 2, 3, 4; composes music, 2, 4, 7, 8, 14–16; responds to climate and nature, 2, 7, 11, 12, 14–15, 16, 17, 136; his journalism, 2, 80, 99,